THE SCHOOL
IN ROSE VALLEY

The Main Building

THE SCHOOL IN ROSE VALLEY

A Parent Venture in Education

Grace Rotzel

with contributions from
teachers, parents, and children

THE JOHNS HOPKINS PRESS

Baltimore and London

This book is dedicated to
Wayne Higley and Donald Clark,
who insisted that it be written
and who are demonstrating these ideas
in larger fields.

CONTENTS

ACKNOWLEDGMENTS

IN MY thirty-six years at The School in Rose Valley there has always been an active group of parents willing to give what it takes to make a school a success. Since these people really make this story, I acknowledge with grateful appreciation their enthusiasm, ideas, good humor, craftsmanship, manual labor, common sense, determination, and most of all, their intelligent understanding. I never found them wanting.

The individual parents, teachers, and children who have contributed to this book illustrate some of these qualities. The school has been a part of them. They have made the book not only more interesting but more representative.

I wish especially to thank Peg Nowell, Wayne Higley, and Margaret Rawson for reading the manuscript and giving valuable suggestions, and also the teachers whose records I have quoted. To all others who have helped and to all my co-workers over the years I am deeply grateful.

Most of all I want to acknowledge my debt to Marietta Johnson, the founder and director of the School of Organic Education in Fairhope, Alabama. It was in my years of working with her that I became convinced of the need for change in education and gained there the confidence to work toward this end.

Dr. Leon Saul, writer of the Foreword, is emeritus professor of preventive psychiatry at the University of Pennsylvania, author of *Emotional Maturity* and other books, and father of two children who went through The School in Rose Valley. His contribution to our maturity is described in chapter 14.

FOREWORD

THIS BOOK traces the development of an idea that began in the imagination of a group of parents and was brought to fruition in The School in Rose Valley. This is the kind of school in which learning became so enjoyable that a child cried if he had to miss a day, a school he wept to leave when his age required departure. It is a school where he absorbed pleasurably so much real knowledge that he could go on to superior accomplishments in the routinized, lock-stepped schools that are so typical of today's educational system.

Why did this school survive and flourish? The answer lies somewhere in the interaction of the parents, the children, and Grace Rotzel, who tells this story. The parents' secret was their intense interest; Grace's secret was that her interests matched theirs. She is a woman whose inner light radiates through all she says and does. Because of this quality she was asked to be the first principal of the school; because of it she attracted like people to the staff, and guided the gleam in the eyes of parents to fruition. This quality was partly her own personality and partly her interest in all of life—her feeling and learning through the feeling and thinking of the children.

The sense of reality in most people is so warped by their past conditioning, training, and teaching that instead of acting on accurate perception, they are largely influenced by prejudice, preconceptions, and opinions, rather than by observation and reason. But Grace Rotzel is a realist, and she stands for education to and through reality. Many academic and theoretical writers have stressed this thought, but Grace has exemplified it and, therefore, so has The School in Rose Valley.

This is the story of a school that stimulates and encourages chil-

xi

dren to follow their own natural impulses of interest, curiosity, and creativity, allowing and helping them to learn by exploring and experimenting in the real world, as well as with books and abstractions. Here the child becomes interested in arithmetic by building, in science by observing and living with animals and trees, in astronomy by trying to create a representation of a solar system, and in art by exercising his own artistic expression. Here he is guided to learn from the real world about animate nature, about himself and about others, as individuals and as groups. Thus he combines book learning, our heritage from the past, and organic experience with the realities of each subject. This is the story of a school that was created to meet the immediate challenges in the education of children, the challenges to understand mankind, himself, and others. Who am I? What shall I learn? Why? Here is the story of how one group of parents, their children, and their environment were put together in constant interaction and how they focused on the essential goals of understanding and of action based on that understanding. Certainly the educational upsurge in the twenties, now followed by a greater upsurge in the sixties, was the result of the questions: Who are we? What are we? What should we do with our lives? How can we create men of good will in a world so rife with repressed hostility, broken homes, crimes, revolutions and wars which have forever plagued mankind? Here, in the search for answers to the really important questions, lies the hope that understanding can and will combat the only real threat to humanity—man himself. If this hope is not to be in vain, then education must be designed to help children face these questions and seek answers on their own levels. This is what The School in Rose Valley has tried to do and why it came into being. Herein is sketched some of its happy story.

LEON J. SAUL

1

THE BEGINNINGS

I WOULD TEACH, I said, but not be the principal. I wasn't a principal kind of person. I didn't like straight lines, so was a poor disciplinarian; I hated fund raising and would certainly be no good in persuading parents to enroll their children.

It was the spring of 1929. A group of Rose Valley parents had been studying child development during the winter; their probings had raised questions about education, and they went to Dr. W. Carson Ryan, head of the Education Department of Swarthmore College, to ask whether the new knowledge they had gained was actually being used by teachers. He suggested that they look around for themselves, which they did. They visited Oak Lane Country Day School in Philadelphia; Shady Hill School in Cambridge, Massachusetts; The Windward School in Scarsdale, New York; Hession Hills in Croton, New York; The Lincoln School, Dalton School, and City and Country School, all in New York City, and they saw a new approach that was exciting; the children were natural, living and learning naturally. It all seemed sensible and genuine. But when they visited the places where their children would go to school, they did *not* like what they saw: it was restricted and uninspiring. Dr. Ryan met with them several times, and finally said, "If you don't like what you see, why not start a school of your own?"

Now, as a possible candidate for principal, I was being interviewed in the Rose Valley home of two of these parents. The group had had many meetings; this was the first I had attended. They were determined to try any suggestion of Dr. Ryan's, and I was one of his suggestions. I was eager to get into this new venture, but my unwillingness to accept responsibility was making it difficult for me to become involved.

1

These Rose Valley parents, like many others, were reacting to the rapid changes of the twenties. Changes which had been given impetus by the disillusioning experiences of World War I. Two of the group, for example, had been conscientious objectors, who most certainly were thinking of a better world for their children. Changes were coming so rapidly in communication, in technology, and in science that it was clear that education must adapt. John Dewey had shown the way; the Freudians were showing the way; and a great many were saying, "Let's get on with it."

Madeline Dixon, the leader of the Lower School at Oak Lane Country Day School where I was teaching the fourth grade, had told me of "an interesting group in Rose Valley. It started as a colony of artists at the beginning of the century. I suggest you find out all you can, and take seriously whatever is offered."

It was a fascinating group that I met when I finally arrived for my interview, and the history of the Valley was as interesting. In 1901 William Price, one of a group of eager-minded Philadelphians, including Edward Bok and the Fels brothers, Samuel and Joseph, was instrumental in organizing the Rose Valley Association, a stock company chartered to encourage handicrafts used in the furnishing of houses.[1]

This was a part of the arts and crafts movement of the times, inspired by Ruskin and Morris. The movement was hastened by the rapid development of factories where the workers felt no relation to the whole product. Talks began about the "whole man" at the same time educational leaders were talking about the "whole child." Five years earlier, in 1896, John Dewey had started the Laboratory School at the University of Chicago, the aim being the "development of human beings in knowledge, understanding and character." Price agreed with Dewey when he wrote about the Rose Valley Association: "This is no mere return to simple or archaic methods of production, but an assertion of the dignity and necessity of constructive work. The importance of this is not so much in the hope it offers of better made things, as it is of a saner life which shall recognize the development and happiness of man as the end of his activities."

With capital of approximately $25,000, including a loan of $9,000 from Swarthmore College, this group bought eighty acres of farmland and two old mills with their surrounding properties along Ridley Creek in Delaware County, Pennsylvania. Here they hoped to offer craftsmen, at union wages and amid pleasant surroundings, the sort of work which would not only produce beautiful objects, but which would also develop the worker.

In one of the mills was a furniture shop. A bookbindery was estab-

---

[1] The details of the history of Rose Valley were given by Eleanor Price Mather, niece of William Price.

lished, as well as a shop for metal work and one for handwrought jewelry; and a noted ceramic artist brought in a group of French potters.

The other old mill became the Guild Hall, where anyone interested in plays (and practically everyone in the Valley was) could meet to act, make scenery, or criticize the current production, which was going on under Price's direction, for, in addition to being an architect, he was a poet, critic, writer, and producer of plays, and he had the warmth and ability to inspire people to use their creative talents. He knew something about everything except finances. The Association was destined to financial failure. Though Rose Valley furniture gained recognition in the world of arts and crafts, it was too expensive and did not sell.

However, the spirit of that venture has lived on in the Valley. Out of it came the still-active Rose Valley Chorus and the Rose Valley Players. The dramatic activity attracted Jasper Deeter, who in 1923 began The Hedgerow, a repertoire theater that is still operating.

With such a background, it is not surprising that those who inherited this spirit should start a school with the idea of developing all of the native capacities of each child, instead of just teaching him how to read, write, and gather facts. When they spoke with me about becoming principal of their school, I was struck by a special quality in them—the certainty that *of course* the ideal and the real could be joined. I discovered that they had no intention of offering the kind of position I had in mind. They were organizing a board with four committees—admissions, finance, education, property— and they intended to surround these functions very thoroughly. This kind of support attracted me to the job they offered. They wanted me to direct the educational program and to teach a group of the children. It sounded exciting, and I became the first principal of The School in Rose Valley.

Dr. Ryan promised to act as director for one year without pay; Dr. Frances Burlingame acted as associate director, and Edith Everett, a special lecturer at Swarthmore, as special advisor on elementary education. The parent committees were to find pupils, a house, and funds, and I was to make plans to put the whole in operation. My only addition to the plan, a request for a shop and shop man, was accepted, and school opened in September, 1929, in the little house where we had our first meetings. This building fitted comfortably the needs of twenty-nine children and five teachers, with its many doors opening on attractive outdoor living space. A large open field was perfect for kite flying, garden making, and various digging operations. At the lower end of the property, under a big willow, large black-spotted orange salamanders lived in the spring that fed a stream full of interesting life, such as caddis worms, back-swimmers, minnows, tadpoles, and snails. The adjacent Geary woods leading down to the

3

marsh was ours also to roam over and investigate, and this, with the stream-bound meadow, made a perfect setting for our school.

The staff of five, with our various backgrounds, learned from each other. Mary Spiller had studied English Nursery Schools for a year. Gertrude Gilmore had worked for a year at the Merrill–Palmer School in Detroit, and as assistant in the Nursery School of Colorado State Teachers College. Esther Wilson had been director of junior work in the Swarthmore Chautauqua. Edward Rawson had been head of Friends Schools and public schools in New York City. He had been instrumental in introducing shop work in these schools, had taught history and mathematics, and had a habit of working for ideas rather than money. He had retired and gone to live with a son in Texas, but when he heard of this school he said, "This is so vitally interesting. I must get in on it," which he did. With all of the vigor of a man who had spent his first sixty-nine years developing interesting ideas, he demonstrated in his last eighteen years his belief that shop work was not just for boys preparing to be carpenters, but for anyone who wanted to make things, which included every child alive, girls as well as boys. Also, we felt that shop work was one of the best ways of developing self discipline in a child.

I had been part-time director of a private school at Valley Cottage, New York. It had taken me a long time and a variety of experiences to become interested in education. Before college, I had had fun teaching in a small rural school and after college I had been a high school English teacher in New York state. It was mostly fun; I was learning how to handle a job, to be part of the community, to chaperon the young, and, of course, to make sure that my students passed their courses. Only after I had a state certificate, had been made head of a department, and had been given some responsibility for writing state regents examinations, did I gain enough confidence to question what was going on in my school. Why did everything have to be so cut and dried? These students were not using half of their capacity. I was sure I was at fault, but wasn't there something wrong with the system, if there was so much dependence on the teacher? Where were the self-starters? Then I read a magazine article by Stanwood Cobb on Marietta Johnson and The School of Organic Education in Fairhope, Alabama.

I enrolled in a summer course at her school in Edgewood, Connecticut, and that fall I began working in her school in Alabama. Marietta Johnson, a dynamic, down-to-earth woman, had been a successful teacher in a normal school in Minnesota when she read *The Development of the Child* by Nathan Oppenheim. "If what this man says is true," she said, "then I am doing the wrong thing." Shortly afterward she established her own school in Fairhope, Alabama, the site of a single-tax colony in which her husband was interested. Here she put into action her new understanding of child development and the ideas of John Dewey.

4

I found the place a revelation. Here were children, from kindergarten through high school, learning because they wanted to, without grades, marks, examinations, or prizes. Like all children, they wanted experience; if some of it was drudgery, they worked at it because they wanted the end result—or let it go until they saw the need.

I was fascinated to see that rewards were completely unnecessary, that, in fact, they often got in the way, because the children interpreted the reward as the reason for doing a job, and concluded that the job itself was not worth doing. On one occasion, our pupils competed in some field sports at the local public school. One of our boys won a prize, which confused a classmate who said, "Why did he get a prize? He won. I think the one who lost ought to have it. He feels bad."

I spent five years at Fairhope. Its atmosphere of openness and freedom, the work-for-work's sake idea, with creativity emphasized as basic instead of peripheral, gave me a whole new outlook on a deeper level of education.

Then, in 1929, this staff of five teachers, with twenty-nine children of founders, friends of founders, and of others who were willing to try something new, started to work in The School in Rose Valley.

Because we wanted the children to have as much freedom as possible, we set up definite schedules for each group. To some this may sound like a contradiction, but those who work with children know that a routine that takes care of big decisions leaves the children freer than if every decision is his to make. Each day the groups had an inside and an outside activity period, a chance at shop, music, language (stories, conversation, dramatization), painting or clay modeling, academic work including science, and some time for relaxation.

In that first year, in addition to everything else, a great deal of building was going on. Mr. Rawson started by making a shop out of an abandoned Sears and Roebuck wooden playhouse. His creation of a shop out of that structure gave us our first inkling that he could make something out of nothing. Well, almost nothing. He doubled its size, added two work benches, and with the addition of a stove, had an adequate workroom. The children were fascinated. Of course, they liked to build, too. The five-years-olds made a brick playhouse that year, a large project that may have represented the teacher's yearnings more than the children's, but they all had fun with it; a year later it had windows, a door and a fireplace. They even wove a rug for it. The six- and seven-year-olds needed a shelter for pets, so they built a "barn," suitable for guinea pigs and a setting hen, and divided it so that each family of animals might have private quarters.

But the crying need was for a classroom for the second year. The oldest group (third and fourth grades) begged to build it, and they did. Here is Mr. Rawson's report as printed in *The Parents' Bulletin*, a monthly news letter:

Two months ago a portion of space back of the school was selected and we are enclosing it with walls, floor, and roof for occupancy by the oldest group next year.

Since the first of March, members of this group have given some time each day to the various kinds of work involved, beginning with digging holes for the foundation posts and including framing timbers, nailing on siding, roofing and painting. When it came to putting up the rafters, I was about to call upon the men of the Property Committee who had offered to help, but the boys thought we could do it ourselves. I thought not, but they said, "How do you know we can't do it? We don't know until we try." As that was just what I had been saying to them all winter in the shop, there was nothing to do but try. We tried and did it, and now the house is all done but— finishing. They didn't like it when I engaged a man to dig the forty foot trench for water pipes, but were reconciled when it was explained that we shouldn't have time to do that and the building too. We did quite a lot of work in the spring holidays.

The new house will have one room, 20′ by 24′, and a smaller one, 10′ by 10′, with folding doors between, a cloak room and two toilets. We shall do the plumbing, too. Unless a better plan is suggested, the large room will be heated by a jacketed stove in the north end, and in the small room will be the stove that will heat the water. There will be plenty of work next fall making closets, shelves, and sundry articles of classroom furniture.

This made us feel sure that we would continue next year, possibly beyond that, while we gave our attention to exploring the environment, working out a curriculum that would encompass children's needs.

An eight-year-old's diary during that first year gives a sample of one child's school experiences:

Dec. 10: I made a block print and only one was good. We made molasses cookies. We put up suet for birds.

Dec. 17: We found a duck that was pecked and took it to the farmhouse. We think a crow did it.

Dec. 20: Today we had the play, and this afternoon we go caroling. We made an Indian village and we have a wattle house.

Jan. 10: We are making experiments to see bacteria grow. We stick a clean thumb and a dirty thumb in jello. It didn't work. It got watery.

Jan. 16: Today the Los Angeles (a dirigible) flew over the school.

Jan. 17: We found two salamanders. We put them in with the brook fish. We have some guppies. They are in the new aquarium.

Jan. 21: We are painting a map of the United States on the floor. One of the salamanders died. It looked as if his tail had been eaten.

6

Jan. 27: The new guppies died. I made a clay pitcher and tore it up. I made another and the handle came off.

Feb. 3: Tra la la, Tra la la. That is what I sing on the way to school.

Feb. 4: We made a dam down at the swamp. We brought up water from the brook. We have caddis worms, dobsons, mosquito larvae, a red salamander and a spotted salamander.

This record confirmed some parents' suspicions that we were walking around outdoors a good deal of the time. We were. But the "Tra la las" meant to us that we were on the right track.

The shop and outdoor activities gave the community its first inkling that this school was different. A building being made by children, and a group wandering along streams with fish nets and pails were visible. "Of course the children are having a good time, but that isn't education! How will they ever pass examinations?" Timid parents removed their children with a minimum of delay; others transferred at the end of the year.

Many visitors, then and in later years, were dismayed by the activity they saw and by the informal nature of the classrooms. Prospective parents usually asked to see the oldest group, for there they could observe children accustomed to the school, and could judge the kind of learning going on. It could be disconcerting if one expected a sober, quiet, studious atmosphere, to find children painting a map on the floor, a few arranging a display on the ceiling, small groups each working on something engrossing, possibly a few doing nothing, but all completely oblivious to noise. Some visitors came away in shock; others with the remark, "If only I had gone to a school like this!" And the usual question arose, "How will they adjust to another school in seventh grade?" In the early days we had to answer that we did not know, but we added that the pupils had managed to adjust to many situations, and we expected them to continue to do so. We were happy to find later that our expectations were borne out. Most of the children met the educational requirements of the public or private schools they attended later with large margins of safety.

In breaking old patterns and making new ones, we had no intention of discarding all traditional subject matter, since much of it was necessary for a child's understanding of himself and the world. The old idea that knowledge was power, was partly true; it was how to *gain* knowledge, and how to *use* it that was important. The concept of what constituted learning was what every teacher had to work on. If memory and obedience were not the most valued assets of a learner, what were? Those qualities enabled him to pass examinations; but we were interested in the whole child, in what goes on as he thinks, acts, talks, and behaves. Learning is the change that takes

7

place as the result of experience, and this was our concern. We had to keep in mind as we planned these experiences that the child is a social being, that he has active urgent interests that need to be considered, and that school is a place where he *lives* instead of a place where he is preparing for the next school.

Two circumstances were valuable in this period. One was that the Depression forced us to remain a small unit, and to learn how to make our own equipment. The other was that at least half of the teachers were mothers, so of necessity we were very close to that other educational institution, the family. Group teachers had to meet professional requirements, and fortunately several mothers were qualified to do so; but there were also various part-time positions which other mothers could and did fill. We cheerfully faced the hazards of having mothers in the same school, for we felt that the advantages outweighed the disadvantages. We usually managed to have mothers and their offspring in separate areas. With the family and the school working on the same principles there seemed to be no limit to what children could do.

2

THE APPROACH TO SUBJECT MATTER

As THE SCHOOL'S STAFF worked together on curriculum in the exciting first years, we also studied child development, so that we could perceive the stages of child growth and provide a balance of freedom and restraint that would encourage inner discipline. We recognized two facts that startled and interested us. First we noted that in the early years children do more than fifty per cent of their physical growing and also a significant percentage of their total learning. Second, we saw that since the active brain centers are largely motor and sensory until the age of seven, the thinking process develops in conjunction with muscles and senses.

Our problem then was to provide an environment in which the child could use his muscles and his senses to initiate action (such as using tools to make something of his own design). When he failed, we wanted the environment to be one in which he could find a way to correct his errors and to succeed—in short, an environment that would help the thinking process along; we needed to provide experiences that would arouse curiosity, stretch muscles, strengthen initiative, and stimulate questions. So we aimed to approach the big concepts (the idea of the solar system, for example) in as many ways as we could devise and to touch on them repeatedly in the early years. We called it first-hand experience.

For instance, here is a *Parents' Bulletin* report in 1930 on how the solar system was introduced:

People visiting the school have wondered about the big eighteen-inch rubber ball in the cedar tree by the shop. That is the center of our solar system. Owen Stephens, Barbara's father, thought out the scheme for us. The fourth grade measured the distances and placed the planets. The first planet, Mercury, is a tiny bead seventy feet

9

from the sun. It hangs on a branch of the beech tree, and like the other planets, has a waterproof label. Venus, a slightly larger bead, is on the maple, one hundred and thirty feet distant. The earth, a bead about the size of Venus, is at a distance of one hundred and eighty feet, and Mars is three hundred feet away down by the chokecherry. The rest of the planets are off the school grounds. Jupiter, a tennis ball, is in an apple tree in Eugene Brewer's yard, approximately one thousand feet from the sun. Saturn, an inch-and-a-half ball, with a cardboard ring, is seventeen hundred feet away in Ned Chandlee's yard. Uranus, a marble, is thirty-five hundred feet distant in Richard Taylor's yard in Media. Neptune is fifty-five hundred feet from school in the yard of James Vail in Media. Planet X (not yet called Pluto) is at Broomall's Dam, seven thousand feet away.

On April 22 the fourth grade, with Owen Stephens as chief explainer, went to Swarthmore to see Jupiter and its moons through the big telescope.

This was the beginning of the study of earth and sky during those first years. There were many variations: night parties to look at the sky; planets painted on the ceiling; planets made of clay; a planetarium of wood, wire, and an electric light, made by a child with Mr. Rawson's help; star boxes, using a light behind pricked slides to show the constellations or an eclipse; and, of course, the most sensible way for a child—acting it out. When children vied with each other to "be" the earth, or sun, or moon, and to show in silent motion which was which, you knew the beginning of a concept had arrived. Next came dancing this concept to music, then adding other planets, and eventually showing a universe of whirling children.

All of the teachers and children were in a new environment that made exploration a natural process. It seemed fitting that geography and history should start with first-hand experience, especially since Rose Valley had an exceptionally interesting history, and a varied terrain with fascinating plant and animal life. We early determined that since we were living in the country, natural science would have to be central in our thinking. Here I was at a disadvantage, for I had never had the benefit of any sort of "course study" of plant and animal life, nor had I learned much about the structure of the earth. To be sure, I had been brought up on a farm, and I remembered one glowing confrontation with a cricket in the rural school I attended. One day the teacher brought one, in a cage made of a lamp chimney and a flower pot, and I must have been deeply impressed, for that afternoon Mother and I went up on the hill at the back of our house and caught crickets. (It is the only thrilling thing I remember about that school.) One of the first things I did in 1929 was to buy a bound volume of the Cornell leaflets (*Handbook of Nature Study*) by Anna Bottsford Comstock, since I couldn't think of a better reference book for the country teacher I was to become.

In high school I had studied the usual Latin, Greek, German,

English, history, Bible, elocution, and physics, but biology hadn't yet arrived. Physics did not give me an understanding of the earth— just definitions and formulas, not even a laboratory. In college I had one course that stands out like the cricket in my memory, and on these two experiences I had to rely. This was a course in physiology and anatomy which required dissection. I was fascinated and inspired by this, my only adventure with planned biology. Fifteen years later, I made use of what I had learned, and longed to know more. Well, I could learn, and why not learn with the children?

I had visions of getting some biologist to build a laboratory on our grounds, so we could have him handy to watch and to answer questions, but this remained merely a vision until five years later. In the meantime, how to go to work? We started by walking, collecting animals (dead or alive), bones, owl pellets. I put up suet for birds. What we wanted was to get acquainted. Feeding birds was one way; but how to get questions asked and answered?

Fortunately my college roommate, Mabel Brown Gillespie, who was now married to an ornithologist, lived nearby, and both she and her husband wrote articles for nature magazines. They offered to sponsor me if I wanted to become a bird-bander, sending to Washington records of birds banded and recovered; they would help me with traps and identification. I sent in my application for a bird-banding license, and began observing birds and making traps. Only persons over sixteen were permitted to be banders, but the children could watch what was going on, keep feeders supplied, and help keep records. The ground trap, frequented by white-throated sparrows and juncos, could be shut by a wire stretched from its door to the window of a classroom. When a child whispered to me, "There's a bird in the trap," I let down the trap door. Then everybody watched me remove the bird, and looked with awesome eyes at the tiny quivering bit of life; maybe a child would notice the black and white stripes on its head and the white patch on the throat, but probably not. Mostly he wondered about anything so small. After the aluminum band, with a number on it, was carefully placed on the bird's leg, and all the required data written down, I opened my hand slowly, with the bird on its back, and gradually he realized his freedom and flew away. We knew he wasn't hurt, because he came back to the ground trap many times, and frequently from the woods came his sweet, far-away song of "pea-bod-y-bird." Chickadees, cardinals, and woodpeckers came to the tree trap and they returned year after year.

Out of this experience came the planting of sunflowers for cardinals, trumpet vines for humming birds, making bird houses for wrens; collecting abandoned nests of cardinals, robins, wood thrushes, chipping sparrows, red-eyed vireos, goldfinches, and catbirds; and making bird games.

11

A field trip

The stream on the school grounds led into Vernon Run, and it flowed into Ridley Creek which meandered down to the Delaware River. There was a fisherman's path along Ridley Creek; following this path on successive walks, once each week, until we reached the river seemed the obvious way to find out where we were, and who else were here—people, plants, animals. Items from a child's diary:

We went for a walk yesterday and it was all rocky. The place we went was Long Point (on Ridley). We came to a spring and took a drink. On the way back we saw a cardinal.
We saw a downy woodpecker with a red top, and then we saw its mate. We counted seventy-nine rings on a tree stump.

Out of this walking along the stream came maps: first on the floor with chalk, the child walking the direction; then on big brown paper on the floor, maps that could be raised to the wall to be semipermanent; later we made relief maps, including one of the school grounds, and one of Rose Valley. And every walk was a collecting expedition for stones, leaves, bones, feathers—anything that attracted our attention.

We tried to find out what Rose Valley was like before we got there, and this gave us some experience with history. We read accounts of the Lenape Indians in Smithsonian pamphlets and missionary records and took trips to the University of Pennsylvania Museum to see the Indian exhibits. We followed the Minquas Trail, marked by a bronze beaver on Rose Valley Road; made a wattle house; and dug for artifacts. (We found only one arrow head, but were sure there was a kitchen midden on Long Point.) We explored more recent history by visiting the Old Swede's Church and Penn's Landing on nearby Christiana Creek, by interviewing the occupants of mill houses at Sackville and Plush Mill (towns close to the school), and by talking with the residents of Rose Valley who were over seventy.

One of the pupils wrote to Dr. Antrim Osborne, a native of the Valley who was then living in California, and asked him for a description of Rose Valley when he was a boy. Dr. Osborne's response was a remarkable six-page letter and a map that he drew to show where, in his youth, he had found turtle eggs, fox grapes, hazel nuts, and wild strawberries. A copy of this letter, which the student made and incorporated into a hand-bound book, is still consulted by those interested in Rose Valley's past.

We watched history in the making that year by following the account of Admiral Byrd's activities in the Antarctic through daily reports in the *New York Times*. The children made a model of the region around Little America, using salt and flour for icebergs; they made models of the Jacob Rupert (one of Byrd's ships), dog sleds, tents, and airplanes; and made dugouts with tunnels leading outdoors. All of this brought the experiences of the men in the Antarctic close to us. Those explorers never knew how much they stretched out imaginations that year; the children felt the cold, enjoyed the mountain climbing, and for one boy, later a navy pilot, Admiral Byrd remained a life-long hero.

Some people were bothered by the obvious differences between our school and conventional ones. We spent "too much time walking around outdoors"; we called teachers by their first names ("there isn't any respect"); we were too permissive ("the children aren't learning anything"); the children can't wait to get to school—there must be something wrong! I was always curious as to why the school seemed to be a personal insult to some, even those who had no children to educate, but gradually I came to accept the fact that any deviation from tradition is seen by some people as a threat. Stories about us ran fast, many of them true. The usual remark to end a horrendous account of happenings at the school was, "What can you expect? There isn't any discipline at all." We always welcomed visitors, but the tale-tellers had not visited—"I wouldn't set foot in the place."

As to first names, at the beginning they just happened. We all had the habit of calling one another by our first names. We felt an informal atmosphere necessary for our ends, and since we felt that

13

respect had no direct relation to what one was called, we decided to let each individual make his own decision as to what he wished to be called. If he felt easier with an appendage to his name we all would oblige. Frequently there were changes: Eloise Holmes started as Mrs. Holmes, but soon was Holmsie. A child in a hurry called Mr. Rawson "Mister" and the other children took up the name; from then on he was "Mister" to everyone. On the other hand, Mr. Freeman was always "Mr. Freeman," for that seemed best for him.

Permissiveness was not a bad word in the thirties, but to some who had misinterpreted the psychiatrists and the progressives it meant abdication of authority. Having worked with Marietta Johnson, I interpreted the word as she did, and it certainly did not mean "anything goes." We thought that our pupils were in the phase of growth where they needed a great deal of support. The adults' job included providing a simple regular routine to supply physical needs, and this required conformity. It meant that there had to be rules. Permissiveness, in the constructive, educative sense that we understood it, means that adults listen to what the child says he wants to do, then, as Marietta Johnson said, "If it isn't physically impossible, or morally wrong, let him do it." The important thing about permissiveness was listening, and, within the routine framework, giving as much freedom as the child could use.

A *Parents' Bulletin* of 1933 gives a sense of our thinking at that time:

The school day is planned with definite thought for the child's needs, and depriving him of any part of this diet is not legitimate any more than depriving a child of some part of his food is legitimate. There is a temptation, if a child is irritable and flighty, difficult with others, to use the threat that he may not go to shop. This should happen only as a very extreme measure, as doubtless shop work is the one thing he needs most. We must never use a child's liking for one subject as a club to beat him into doing something else. Each subject has its own reason for being.

Also it is well to keep in mind the long-time task on which you are working. Do not expect the child to be made over in a week or two. If he has started with fear habits, it takes a long time to build a new attitude toward the world. In the meantime the child is first very docile, then very "uppity," and finally, after many months, possibly years, he becomes a poised, clear-headed child. During the process of breaking old habits and making new ones, he is likely to be a tremendous nuisance. But if you can keep your mind on the process that is going on, and not be too concerned with the immediate present, the chances for education are good.

On the matter of social engagements: There is a tendency to pattern children's lives on the adult plan, with luncheon engagements, afternoon dances, musicals and dramatics. The first recommendation we make is that the social calendar be simplified as much as possible. Children need to be alone some of the time. They need to be thrown on their own resources. For six hours during the school day they have companions at work and play. This is stimulating and delightful, and they like to prolong it by afternoon visiting. A limited amount of this is good, but every child should have a quiet hour or two to himself every day. The objection is sometimes raised that children are bored if left alone. If so, there has been something wrong with their education, and they need to be bored. If they are so lacking in resources that they cannot entertain themselves, they are in an unhealthy state and a diagnosis should be made. Dancing, dramatics, music lessons should be a part of the school curriculum, and an integral part of the day. Besides, a dramatic club often defeats its own end, for the plays are put on by adults with children saying the lines. Children should work out their own plays.

The School in Rose Valley does not give entertainments for adults. The children give plays and other programs for each other, and talk frequently in Assembly before an audience of their peers. There is no posing, and the interest is in the subject. An adult audience puts an unnatural strain on children, which all too often results in "showing off."

While practising constructive permissiveness and seeking to simplify the lives of the children, we began using the resources of our environment. Our subject matter ranged from the spider web in the corner to Planet X, and happily the foundation laid in these first years has been a good cornerstone for later programs. To children the immediate environment is all important, and must be understood; but as educators we felt that it must also lead out into larger areas with no limits of time or space. One of the exciting things about this approach was that the teachers were learning along with the children.

15

3

A QUESTION OF SURVIVAL

NOT LONG AFTER we established the school, the Department of Education at Swarthmore College was discontinued. I could not help regretting the timing of that administrative decision, for Dr. Ryan of that department had been a comforting source of advice and help.

Lack of money was a shock, too. Though the School in Rose Valley was conceived and born in the affluent twenties, it was short of money from the beginning. Dr. Ryan had warned the founders of our school that starting it would be more expensive than they had imagined. He suggested that they should not consider it unless they could guarantee a budget of $16,000, or $400 tuition for each of forty children. Since the highest tuition in the area was $150, it was out of the question to find forty children with parents able and willing to pay $400 a year tuition. Dr. Ryan also emphasized the wisdom of equal tuition for all ages, based on commensurate needs. He pointed out that because the early childhood years, where learning habits are formed, are most significant in the educational process, the teachers of the youngest should have exceptionally good training and experience, and further, that a smaller tuition for three-year-olds would support the idea that nursery school was merely a baby-sitting convenience, a prevalent notion that it was our duty to counteract.

The parents could not meet the recommended budget, but started anyway with what they had—twenty-nine children instead of forty, and $250 tuition instead of $400—and not all parents of the twenty nine paid the $250; some paid part in service. During the first year the money problem was not acute. The school was incorporated in 1930; we had a small budget and a small building fund for the new classroom. The Depression had not yet seeped into our thinking. For the second year we took on a new teacher from the University of Chicago. That meant five regular teachers and two part-time. It was a wonderful year educationally, but we had a firm hard slap financially that brought us up with a start. At the end of that year the Depression submerged us with a deficit of more than half the budget. We had gambled on a sizable increase in enrollment and just thirty-nine pupils turned up. We lost, and the new teacher had to leave.

In our third year, enrollment decreased. The loss of pupils could be explained. In some cases the reason was financial; in others it was the parents' disaffection with anything remotely experimental, or an uncertainty about anything new (Will it last? Will it prepare my children for their educational future? Shouldn't we save the money for college?) In other cases it was definite disagreement with our program. "My four-year-old needs more direction." We had said this child had been given too much direction and needed to have time to direct himself. We were sympathetic with these parents; they had genuine reasons for withdrawing their children and the children couldn't flourish if their parents were worried.

The staff persisted optimistically, with the help of underwriting by Adele and Maurice Saul, and agreed for the time being to accept seventy-five per cent of their salaries. The Board made a minimum, medium, and optimum plan for the year, of which we adopted the minimum. We referred nursery school applicants to an approved nursery school in the area, to which we gave educational support, but no money. We took on two inexperienced teachers and found that inexperienced teachers have advantages; they do not have habits to unlearn, they come with a fresh approach and questions that need to be asked, and they can be a genuine asset when given the needed guidance and practical help.

We were steadied by the fact that the founding parents, whose children started in the youngest group and remained in the school, held fast to their educational insight and common sense. They reacted positively under the leadership of Robert Spiller, president of the Board, by undertaking long-term planning for:
  a. the kind and degree of financial support possible;
  b. the location, kind, and size of a permanent plant;
  c. the tuition scale and age range of the student body;
  d. the salary scale for teachers; and
  e. the range and variety of curriculum.
The Depression, however difficult, had some advantages. The stringent change from the twenties gave us time to consider what values were basic; it challenged us to find resources within ourselves, and made us examine and evaluate our actions and our theories every step of the way. A tenet of the school was that parents should be

17

vitally connected with its problems, and during the Depression this parent-school relationship was unavoidable. In 1933 the tuition exchange plan was instituted. The school established a scale of hourly rates for parents working at the school, from 75¢ an hour for lunch-getting, housekeeping, clerical services, etc., to $3.00 an hour for specialists in art, music, science, etc. This system of employing parents of our pupils helped us gather an understanding group who were working on the same basic ideas at home and at school—an optimum climate for the development of the children. The School in Rose Valley came to be known as a place where parents could work and were needed. Difficulties sometimes arose when mother and child were working too closely, but in the majority of cases these problems were resolved satisfactorily; whenever possible we saw to it that mother and child did not work in the same room.

Our permanent well of enthusiasm, Dr. W. Carson Ryan (who had gone to Washington to be Commissioner of Indian Affairs for the Department of the Interior) wrote: "I am more convinced than ever of the significance of the School in Rose Valley. It is certainly one of the few new good schools in the United States. Its small size blinds us to its real importance—we are likely to forget that in small units like this, feasible for any community, lies the real solution." This buoyant message lifted our spirits and gave us energy to meet the hard decisions of that year.

After five years, the land and building that had been loaned to us were being sold. The depressing prospect of having to move to a new site was balanced by a very real possibility of closing the school. Money was tighter than ever, land was very expensive, and foundations that we interviewed made it clear that they were giving only for adult education. At one of a series of meetings to review educational and financial matters, I made the following speech which summarized our views and aspirations:

One word will sum up the principles that underlie the School in Rose Valley. That word is integrity. I am not using it in any negative sense of goodness, but in the original meaning of the word. An integer is a whole number, or complete entity. Integrity is the state of being whole. A whole child has poise, sincerity, alertness and physical vigor. Lacking these, he lacks integrity.

He may know how to read, do sums, play the piano, and entertain adults; but if he lacks sincerity and independence of mind, or a good sound body, his growth is not healthy; he is not gaining in integrity, and therefore his education is wrong. This definition of education is generally accepted by teachers and parents everywhere. That is, it is accepted as a definition, but it is a long way from being accepted in practice.

There are a large number of parents and teachers who would be willing to sacrifice a great deal of poise and sincerity if only their children would show off well. And not a few who wouldn't worry if their children were pale and anemic if they would only read and

18

enjoy the best books. The task of a school then is to keep constantly in mind the picture of a whole child and to see that growth is balanced.

What does this mean in the planning of a curriculum? It means turning upside down the notions of the traditional school and beginning at the opposite end. We start with activity. The shop is the center of the school. With lumber and tools and an intelligent man who can meet children's needs, the school has made the first important step toward providing a growing environment.

There are several reasons why this kind of activity is so important. First, the physiological laws of growth. The large muscles must get exercise. If they do not get it, if the child is flabby and soft, his nervous system is affected. He is inclined to be peevish and temperamental.

That is the first reason why we consider a shop important. The second is that working with tools furnishes one of the best educational disciplines a school can offer. Up to this point in a child's life, his discipline has come almost always from some person emotionally close to him. It is entirely bound up with a person. With things like tools, he is free to impose his own discipline. He wants the result, or frequently, in a very young child, he merely wants the satisfaction of the act of sawing or hammering. In any case, the desire to make things is so general in children that they are willing to go through much hard work to reach their ends. It is noticeably true that flighty children are less flighty in shop. This is discipline.

Of course, if activity is the center of our curriculum, then reading, writing, and arithmetic can not be. Two things cannot occupy the same place. It is what we said five years ago and we are still saying it. It scared people then and will probably continue to scare. It would be a very limited curriculum indeed that had the three R's as its sole aim.

The three R's are tools to be mastered, but they are means and not ends. When and where they should be acquired must depend upon the child's needs. It would be as silly to say that school exists to teach the three R's as that man exists to make money. Just because the world is a bit bottom-side-upish at present we are not convinced that money is *the* goal, and that man's life is merely the getting of it. It should not be. Well, so with these learning tools that we have to acquire in school. We have to get them, but education is a great deal more than that. It is living and experiencing and stretching mind and body and spirit.

At this point it might be well for me to say that the three R's are taught, that regular standard achievement tests are given, and that our children test satisfactorily in comparison with those in other schools. We plan, however, that the first three years of school life, granted that children are entered at four, shall be freely active, and that books shall be left for the most part until the seven-year-old year.

This is what having integrity as a foundation does in the matter of division of time in our curriculum. Not only shop, but cooking, clay modeling, painting, rhythms, piano playing, singing, all are very important in a well-rounded school life. They are not extras but basic needs.

The necessity for integrity dictates a policy concerning treatment of children. It eliminates marks. If you want your child sincere, you will not confuse him with bribes, marks or blue ribbons. The reward

19

eliminates the educational value; it takes attention away from the intrinsic reason for doing the act, and sets up an artificial reason. Confusion results. The child then accepts the artificial reason for the real one, and tries only those activities with rewards attached. The freedom from dependence upon someone else's standards demands that all adults be careful in the way approval and disapproval are bestowed.

Every child's work is displayed, not merely the best of the group, and every child is made to feel that his best work is worthwhile. What we are after is a sturdiness of mind that insists on living on its own standards that grow with the child.

Since integrity is our main concern, it is obvious that treating children rationally and keeping them in a simple environment are important. So much for theory. What have we actually done? You who have lived with the children can say more accurately than we can what has been accomplished; but I can tell you what we have been working on. There are certain fundamental conceptions that every child should get early in life.

The necessity of putting forth effort. The visitor in our school remarks that there are no toys. There are none, except those that might be considered as tools. The reason for this is that children stretch their imaginations and their muscles much more if they have to create their own toys. Besides, it is important that the child learn early that the world was not made for him, that he has to do something about it. So-called perfect equipment can be inhibiting.

The respect for hand labor. The ability to see the beauty in a piece of hard wood, in a simple clay bowl, to appreciate what it means in painstaking effort to sand that wood or shape that bowl is important as the beginning of artistic training. It is possible to acquire this knowledge superficially in a society where hand-made things are usually expensive, but you can never really know the value of them until you have had some experience at first hand.

A conception of the world about him. It is important that every child get a fundamental conception of comparative anatomy and the interrelations of animal life. All, or most, stray dead animals that are brought to school are opened and the insides examined. Sometimes the skeletons are saved. Collecting bones is encouraged so that we may see the points of similarity.

Familiarity with the laws of plant growth. We not only grow things such as wheat, rye, clover, and vegetables on our "farm" and in gardens, but we are constantly carrying on growing experiments indoors, with different soils, differing conditions of water and sun. The school plans eventually to have a garden containing specimens of every kind of wild flower that grows in this section.

Familiarity with animal life of meadow and stream. Every room has aquaria and terraria, and children are encouraged to have individual ones. All the children know from experience the cycle of tent caterpillar and praying mantis, and individuals know those of toad, salamander, frog, Japanese beetle, cricket and grasshopper.

A fundamental conception of number. Children use yardsticks and rulers, ounces and pounds, quarts and pecks before they learn that six and six are twelve. They use fractions, multiply and divide, and only after they have learned what numbers mean do they begin to treat them abstractly.

A fundamental conception of the universe. This is so important that we take considerable time for it, preferably when the child is eight years old. To learn the earth's place in the universe, the simple facts of the solar system, the motion of stars and planets, to know some of the theories of the beginning of the world, and of the beginning of life and the development of it, this is essential to understanding. The child should have his introduction to it early as a basis for all science and history.

A conception of geography and history as subject matter to be derived from the environment. Following Ridley Creek to the river and to its source, visiting the mills along the way, furnishes the basis for understanding this particular lay of land and the means by which contours of land have shaped men's lives. To write a history of Rose Valley, gleaned from stories of old people in the Valley gives a conception of history not as something in a book, but as something real that has happened, accounts of which do not always agree.

An understanding of what constitutes good art. This is worked on in two ways: first, the literature, drama, and songs are chosen for some literary or artistic excellence, or because they are authentic folk lore; second, the creative work done in music, painting, dancing is unhampered by artificial standards.

The parents at this meeting believed in integrity, too, which meant meeting obligations, but they had not yet recovered from the setback of two years ago. The atmosphere was heavy with pessimism until one of the parents, arose with a question. "Why not build a schoolhouse ourselves? We have the time. We built the stage in this mill for the Gilbert and Sullivan Chorus, and working all night, with women feeding us beans and coffee, was an experience I look back on with pleasure." This suggestion, harking back to the old Rose Valley do-it-yourself-and-have-some-fun idea, was all that was needed. Plans began in earnest, and when people left that meeting the predominant feeling was, we *can* do it.

In December, pledges showed $4,135, a sum representing sacrifices and conviction from about twenty families. Owen Stephens and Craig Janney, both architects, asked to plan a building, said the cost could be cut to fit the $4,000 figure; Adele and Maurice Saul offered to loan the school three acres of land on which to build; and so the Board authorized the construction of a building to be ready by September, 1934.

As soon as the frost was out of the ground in March, weekend work began on the 900-foot ditch to bring water to the orchard site. It was a test of muscles and endurance, but on raw spring days as well as on balmy ones, men, women, and children were out there, men digging and laying pipe, women offering gingerbread and coffee, children playing around, and everybody eating lunch under the apple trees. Only a small percentage of fathers were technically equipped—professors of Sanskrit, literature, finance; artists; lawyers; researchers—they all wheeled barrows of cement, laid foundation blocks, nailed on roof and siding; their wives and older children helped. No labor was hired except the bulldozing for the basement.

21

A "Putter Day"

The plumbing was installed by one whose regular work was designing medical instruments for the Johnson Foundation; the building was wired by fathers who worked for the Philadelphia Electric Company; and a heating system was put in by a father in the furnace business. Work continued from March until September on the thirty-five by ninety foot structure called the Main Building. It was incomplete at the opening of school but the weather was mild, the building usable, and fathers continued to work weekends well on into the winter to finish it. Also, during that fall, Mr. Rawson and the children took down the Mushroom, the classroom they had built at the old site, and erected it as The Chip (off the old block) at the new location. In this, the first of many building projects, we learned that we could have what we wanted if we wanted it enough, and, in addition, that building in itself offered a more interesting experience than we had dreamed possible.

By June 1935, we were on the way. The budget was encouraging; there was a small manageable deficit. We were living under our own roof, which meant continuity for at least five or ten years. We could start some of the projects for which we had been waiting.

4

PRESCHOOL

SINCE THE SCHOOL STARTED with the concept of education as growth, we planned the preschool, where the most growing was going on, with definite but flexible routines and with free areas in which the children could develop habits of independent work. In the early years we provided no toys, just the raw materials—blocks, wood, clay, paint, with tools to use them; and outdoors we had ropes, ladders, and trees. The following excerpt from a teacher's weekly report gives a glimpse of how it went:

WEEK OF OCTOBER 19—GROUP I AGES 2 AND 3   10 CHILDREN

Few tears; no tantrums. Nobody hurt this week. Wednesday six children working with blocks stayed with them as follows: Emma 45 minutes; Katy 35; Johnny 30; Ronnie 20; Joe 15; Billy 10. The quality of work was in proportion to time spent. Last year Emma, for four or five months, rarely stuck with anything for more than five minutes. After we became aware of this trait, we kept her at one job for fifteen minutes every day, until she knew how it felt. She must have liked it.

Outdoors everything down to the twigs on the ground had hard and intelligent use. In music, there were moments when everybody was participating; there was no pressure, merely the offering of an interesting thing and an occasional suggestion. Work with paint and clay was freer and lasted longer. More paint got in hair and mouths but also more got onto paper in varied forms; clay work showed more variety.

Then followed statements on individual problems and this question: "These children kept three adults busy all morning. Are we giving them too much attention? Doing too many things for them? Anticipating too many bumps and falls? We'll try tapering off and see what happens."

23

When the teachers had in hand six weeks of each others' reports, they met together over tea to discuss what they had been doing, what they meant by the terms they had used such as "independence" and "attention spans," as well as to discuss procedures that would be useful to encourage growth in our preschool children.

Due to our small enrollment we had, for a long time, two preschool groups, the two- and three-year-olds and the four- and five-year-olds. A good educational relationship could be built up during two years spent in the same place with the same teachers, and the companionship and mutual help of older and younger children aided learning.

The two preschool groups were discontinued in 1945 when increased enrollment made it necessary to have three classes. Now the three-year-old group was limited to fifteen, the four-year-olds to eighteen, and the five-year-olds to twenty. At that time we began an all-day program with lunch and naps, and a summer program for ages three to twelve.

We had some misgivings about keeping the youngest group until three o'clock, but decided to try it. The decision was made partly because the three o'clock hour was convenient for many of the families, but also we were aware that some of the most important learnings—following a routine, learning to eat, becoming adept at relaxing enough to sleep—often became entwined in emotional conflicts between mother and child, with the child trying to wield power over his mother, and sometimes forming a resistance pattern that continued to be troublesome for years. At school, controls were not emotional; no one was bothered by non-eaters; you expected the child to eat, but if he didn't that was all right. It was fun to be with friends, eat what they were eating, get out your own cot, learn the pattern of relaxing.

Much to our surprise, mothers began telling us that the children came home at three o'clock in much better shape than formerly, when they had come home at eleven-thirty. They were in good spirits and easier to get along with. The reason was obvious: lunch and nap followed quickly after strenuous work, instead of after a long ride home (more children were now coming from a distance). Thus we began the all-day program for all preschool groups, though our rooms were crowded and not well adapted. It is amazing how material circumstances do not matter when one decides on a program of action. Many years later we *did* get a preschool building with three large sunny rooms opening onto three separate playgrounds, with many opportunities for each age group to visit and interact with children of other ages.

Some years later we adopted the Developmental School Placement program devised by Dr. Frances Ilg of the Gesell Institute of Child Development. She and her colleagues discovered in the thirties that a common cause of school failure was immaturity. Because of

24

individual children's differing rates of development, chronological age was not a good single criterion of school readiness. In thirty years of work with young children, Gesell, Ilg, and their staff established behavior norms on certain tasks at half-year intervals up to six years of age, and yearly from six to ten, forming a framework of *average* developmental rate against which each individual child can be compared. On these tests no child passes or fails, but each responds in a manner characteristic of a certain developmental age. Boys generally develop more slowly than girls, especially during the first ten years; we used five and one-half as the optimum age for boys entering kindergarten, and five for girls. This change in admission policy, entering the youngest at three and one-half, and so on, with boys entering first grade at six and one-half, and girls at six, was welcomed by the staff and by most of the parents, as fitting in with our over-all school policy that the child should have plenty of time to go at his own speed, and thus to feel sure of himself in self-initiated activities.

There are always some who argue that the superior child is not well-served by such a system, but we feel, on the contrary, that *he* needs it most. The response of a superior child when he is free to act at his behavioral level is often surprisingly mature; for this reason adults are tempted to place him with older children and then are baffled when his personality and performance seem to suffer. Our observation has been that the superiority is likely to show in verbal areas, and the child is likely to lean on his superior verbal performance and to become proportionately less skillful physically and socially. This does not mean that in time he will not be (or could not be) superior in these aspects, too. The neurological foundation is usually there and simply needs to be encouraged to develop by experiences that keep him eager mentally, physically, and spiritually.

What kind of experiences? First of all, they must be experiences with which the child can cope. He must feel good about himself if he is going to manage his lively bundle of senses, emotions, imagination, curiosity, and powerful physical urges, most of the time. Failures can be surmounted if he trusts himself and others. Teachers and parents must consider this in planning experiences (and sometimes in handling quite unplanned experiences).

Thus, two teachers gave examples in the *Parents' Bulletin* of how they treated aggression:

At the beginning of the year two three-year-old boys looked each other over. The smaller boy lunged at the larger and punched him. The larger threw the other to the ground. He got up and lunged at the larger child again with the same result. The smaller boy got up, looked the other up and down, then said, "Let's go climb on the jungle gym."
Then there is the child who races in and gives the teacher a punch. This is his way of saying Hello.

A little girl sees another with a toy she wants and tries to take it away. The normal action is for the child to hold on and hit the intruder.

Several boys were wrestling and chasing each other. The most aggressive child came over and said, "Stop that fighting!" One of the participants answered, "You don't have to play rough if you don't want to, but if you want to, it's okay." This was acceptable to all and they went on wrestling.

Recently four boys were bickering over a monkey rope. I made a couple of suggestions, neither of which they took, then decided to let them solve it. I stated that I felt they could work it out, and left. When I looked back later they were taking turns, laughing happily.

These examples show how children communicate, and in none of these incidents did the teachers interfere. We feel that children must have many opportunities to express their emotions in order to learn how to handle them. Trusting the children is very important.

What can we do to help a child blow off and ease his angry feelings? I look to the ideas offered by the children in my group this year: "tear paper," "cut with scissors," "pound clay," "do angry dancing," "sit in your locker," "hammer wood." We trust the children in being able to play and generally work out relationships.

We found that animals helped children emotionally. Animals and children belong together, and the more kinds of animals the better; they were a bond throughout the school. Guinea pigs with their frustration-proof nervous systems were good for young children who needed something to handle and love. A homesick child forgets his troubles with a guinea pig to hold, and as his interest grows, he helps to care for it. A duck, rabbits, bantams offered variety for the older pupils. What we thought was a duck turned into an aggressive drake that attacked legs, especially those with stockings. Petey, the rooster, had his tail pulled out by a dog. Although Petey and the hens belonged to the first grade, the hen house and its occupants seemed to belong to the younger children, too. When Petey was finally killed by a dog, the preschoolers mourned him with the six-year-olds. The children made a moving occasion of the burial, marching and singing to give vent to their emotions. Fortunately, on the same day, the children discovered that two fluffy chicks had just hatched. It did not always happen that way, but in any event, grief was shared. However difficult the loss, we felt it was better for the child to express it than to store it up for nightmare material in weeks ahead. Emotion unexpressed may emerge as anger, something to cope with. One way to help children cope is to maintain an attitude of openness to unhappy as well as happy experiences; such open frankness on the part of adults helps to give children a firm sense of reality. Singing, dancing, composing stories and songs have been activities by which children expressed what they felt.

Young children delight in the nonverbal communication of rhythms and pantomime. Often the music period was used for the rhythmic acting out of some idea for others to guess; when they can share this

26

Concentration

kind of activity with older children so much the better. I remember an incident when the eleven-year-olds made this announcement in assembly: "We think the youngest children have been very good about listening to all our reports about Egypt, and probably they weren't interested in them or in our play. So this morning we are acting out Phil's poem just for them." The poem went like this:

Johnny Went Out Hunting

Johnny got his pop-gun
And Johnny got his hound
And Johnny went out hunting bear
With snow upon the ground
And he walked
   And he walked
      And he walked
         And he walked
Just   like   this!

and so on for many hair-raising stanzas, all illustrated in pantomime. The preschool children loved it, and when the eleven-year-olds came to their building to take dictation of news and stories they were more than eager, and later listened to their stories read from *Leaves*, the school magazine, with big-eyed pleasure.

Sometimes we separate emotional growth from intellectual growth

27

in our thinking or discussions, but in reality they go together. A child has to feel good about himself and his relationship to people and things if he is to do a good job of investigating, which involves thought; and if he is growing normally, his interests will spark the learning process and keep it going indefinitely if the environment is right.

What then was offered to preschoolers for intellectual stimulation? Raw materials—blocks for outdoors and in, wood, clay (lots of it), paint (the bright clear poster paints with good brushes), and mud, and tools of shop, laboratory, and kitchen. Blocks were a very satisfactory material. At three a child might build a tower, later add a road, and very gradually join another child in some small scheme. This beginning of construction, at four and five grew into group projects that required trial and error, attention to details and relationships. The child had to adapt his impulsive actions to the material and to other builders. From building alone he came to the point where he could say, "I have an idea about that. Can I connect my building to yours?" A typical lay-out of blocks by four- and five-year-olds included a *network* of roads, train tracks, bridges, stations, switches, docks, mills, roundhouses, ships—in fact a system of business and transportation, all interacting.

One staff report mentions continually changing outdoor construction, houses in trees, and those made out of hollow blocks and packing cases, which are miraculously always being finished and always being begun; digging holes, which range from simple holes to drainage systems from rainspouts, to a complicated system of waterways, run and controlled by all the five-year-olds, dredged and filled to hold boats made in shop.

Such schemes suggest trips of which there were many, but trips were not an end in themselves. The questions asked and answered, the discussions back at school of what the children had seen, and the attempt to use their observations as they worked, were the part that meant learning.

Shop was the center of the school, a busy place. Mr. Rawson expected a child to have an idea of what he wanted to make; when a three-year-old came in wanting a derrick that worked, Mister showed him how to start and helped him with the pulley and string until he had something usable. It was harder to satisfy the small girl who wanted to make "a house with a view," but she made one that pleased her. Children naturally start with bigger ideas than they can carry out, but they learn from the consequences. They make mistakes and miscalculations, but they find ways to make corrections. "Why doesn't my stool stand up straight?" (*"Good question. See if you can figure it out."*) Another child gets another kind of pleasure; this one, after working with complete absorption for a long time, looked up with a smile and said, "This is a Fiddle Dee Dee!"

28

In addition to the regular supplies, we collected what we called useful junk—odds and ends from all over—tin, wooden boxes, glass jars, spools, leather scraps, canvas, wheels—in fact we said to parents, "If you are throwing anything away, let us know. We can probably use it." There was always a pile of used lumber available for tree-houses, pet cages, and such.

As the possibilities of raw material were realized, the attention spans increased; mixing colors suggested all kinds of fascinating combinations to use in pictures, and if fingers could do the painting instead of brushes, so much the better; in shop the child discovered that he could make a variety of boats, not just one kind; he could also make what he needed, a pickaxe for digging, for example.

The most arresting and fascinating subject matter came from the earth outside our doors, from the woods, Ridley Creek and its rivulets, the Saul meadow, gardens, and barns, and Lucie Stephen's flower beds. Our unsprayed orchard meant wasps and stings in the fall, but it also meant apple sauce, cider, and maybe apple butter made over an outdoor fire. More than that, it provided good climbing trees. The first trip of the three-year-olds' was often to get sycamore seed balls, or to find acorns, or sweet gum balls, or beechnuts, all within easy walking distance; thus the beginning of talking about seeds.

In the spring there were always a few tent caterpillars, that

The shop

29

hatched from eggs laid on the tips of the branches of our apple trees. From the little children's point of view these brightly colored hairy worms were a bonanza; they made pets of the caterpillars or tried to, until in June the insects crawled away and made cocoons.

The child's natural urge to explore usually meant that specimens were brought in. "I've got a mother cricket (*long tail*). Can I keep it?" "See, my caterpillar fits my sweater." (Both were green.) The young have sharp eyes and can ask more questions than adults can answer, but that was expected. I discovered early that it was not a misfortune that we were all a bit uninformed about natural science, for learning along with the children (and from them) kept us in intimate touch with the learning process.

Getting acquainted with life forms meant more than merely *recognizing* them. For example, we discovered that if we gave the female praying mantid a terrarium fitted to her needs, and supplied her with live insects for food (no easy task) she might make her egg cases while we watched. Also, we found out that if the young were to hatch at the right time for them to have insects to eat, the egg case had to be kept outdoors (another cage to make). If it were left inside in a warm room, one day hundreds of baby mantids would hatch, only to die for lack of food.

While we had to cope with yellow-jackets and poison ivy, most of the life forms around us were beneficent, and we deciphered what we could of the life stories of box turtles, salamanders, crickets, galls, mud wasps, earthworms, grasshoppers, ants, numerous birds, and whatever else we could find.

It was not so much the *names* of the bits of life brought in that interested us (though that was important), but the habits of observation that the children formed. How is this horse chestnut like an acorn? How different? Is the earthworm like the wooly bear worm? Different? A hen's feather and a chestnut shell? Shiny beetle and a piece of mica? and so on.

The job to be done in school at any age is to keep children eager, good-tempered, and healthy. We tried to keep them living hard without forcing, to give them freedom—with a fence around it. We provided structure, but of such a nature that there were ever-widening periods in which a child could initiate his own activity. It is not fair to direct a child all the time, for this inhibits growth toward independence and self-reliance, qualities he must have if he is to mature normally.

5

___

SCIENCE

I N 1934 A NEW FAMILY in Swarthmore, the Herbert and Jean
Ashtons, arrived to enroll their two boys in the school. During
the interview to find out to what activities the parents could contribute, Jean Ashton mentioned that she had taught college biology.
Not only did she have a doctorate from Massachusetts Institute of
Technology but she felt, as we did, that the elementary school was a
strategic place, the place where thinking habits are formed, and
where children are free to feel, listen, see, smell, taste, explore. All
knowledge, but especially science, she said, should be approached in
an exploratory manner. She added that she had a book for children
under way. It was on physiology and anatomy, and included directions for work that could be carried on in any kitchen or classroom;
it even included directions for the dissection of organs found at a
meat market. Now she wanted to work with children on the material
—and could she have a job? There was my scientist in the flesh
asking for a job! This was probably the beginning of my feeling
over the years that someone would come walking down the school
lane to fill our needs, no matter how complicated or impossible they
seemed.

Jean Ashton became our science teacher. She continued working
at The School in Rose Valley until 1941, and during those years she
became an integral part of every classroom.

Adjoining the shop was a room that we had abandoned as a music
room because the piano didn't act well in the basement. This room
was fitted out for science. We put in bunsen burners and other
apparatus, hot and cold water, a blackboard, shelves, books, tables,
etc. It was amazing how much that tiny room, which on rainy days
had to be the passageway to the shop, meant to us all. This was

31

partly because Jean, a connoisseur of coffee, ground coffee there and with scientific precision made the best brew anybody ever tasted. The science room became a staff after-lunch retreat. It was a room, belonging to us all, where interesting things were going on, where one could experiment.

That was what we needed. In our exploration of the environment we had delved into the lives of the earth's inhabitants with considerable interest. This was reflected in the children's writing. But what Jean gave us, in her work on anatomy, as well as in general science, was a scientific approach, a way of thinking, a way of asking questions. Naming and interpreting were not the main objectives in our science work, but seeing likenesses and differences, observing carefully, over and over again. These were important. Since this over-and-over-again technique—observing, asking questions, then more observations, more questions and and more checking—is the child's normal method, it is easy to apply. If this is encouraged, and he finds out something for himself, his natural curiosity is kept alive, and he is helped to formulate his own questions and find satisfying ways of answering them; he is, in effect, working as a scientist works. If, on the contrary, the emphasis is on the right answer, with no concern for the process, he accumulates facts, but neither the ability nor the desire to go farther on his own.

In the thirties, science in the elementary grades was rare, indeed. It seemed too messy for children as well as for teachers; besides, learning, by tradition, consisted of memorizing facts printed in books. But educational thought in the thirties was changing, prodded by such works as Alfred North Whitehead's *Aims in Education*. Whitehead described education as an exciting adventure which should proceed in a rhythm that fitted the stages of mental development. He challenged the idea that easier subjects should precede the harder ones; on the contrary, he said, some of the hardest must come first because nature so dictates, and because they are essential to life. The process of educational growth comes in three stages—ferment, precision, generalization. In general, he maintained, *the elementary school age is the age of ferment, of discovery and exploration.* That statement leaped out of the page at us, for it spoke of our daily experience. Jean Ashton's work with children gave a sense of Whitehead's meaning when he wrote: "this period is the true age for romance of science. The pupils should see for themselves and experiment for themselves, with only fragmentary precision of thought."

Whitehead also wrote of "getting hold of the subject matter as it occurs in nature." An example of how Jean did just this was her tree adoption plan. Each child of a beginning group adopted a tree on the school grounds to be his during all the changes of fall, winter, and spring. Labeling was of relatively minor importance (except that the label was made in shop), for the trees were remembered as

"Billy's that had three kinds of leaves," or "Chip's that had those big sticky buds." The shape, color, and texture of buds, fall colors, the designs of leaf scars, the order of blossom and leaf appearance, birds' and insects' nests found in the trees, fruits, seeds, tiny leaves—all were subject matter for continued discovery. They were all useful for developing habits of observation.

Jean combined experiments with questions to enlist thinking. For example, when ice cubes are put in a dry jar, the outside becomes wet. Why? Like most teachers she was tempted to explain at once, but this would not encourage thinking by the children. If the answers were, "It came through the glass," or "over the top of the glass," the challenge came: "What could you do to prove it did or did not come from the glass?" *Try it.* If some were unconvinced, she would leave it alone for a time and later present the problem in a different way.

One day there was mist on the inside of the window, so she brought up the question of how it got there. Then if a child told her next morning, "I was wondering about that when I went to bed last night," she knew that thinking was going on. This is a good sign for a teacher of any subject, for when some school learning crops up in night time wondering, or in free play, or in conversation, the teacher knows it is gradually becoming usable to the child and a part of him.

Jean's major contribution was her development of the idea that children can learn about their own anatomy by dissection of ordinary market products—hen, rooster, calf's head, sheep's heart and lungs, pig's stomach, calf's pancreas, sheep's liver and kidney. With sketches and detailed directions designed for ten- to twelve-year-olds to use in their own kitchens after they had dissected with a teacher, her book was an excellent introduction to human anatomy. It was of unfailing interest to children, but not to all teachers and mothers. Before Jean came, I had dissected stray animals, and one mother protested my dissection of a squirrel killed by an automobile. She said that I was encouraging brutality and making monsters of the children. My answer was to ask her to be present to watch the next time I dissected, and to listen to the children's conversation. She came, listened, and changed her mind. She later admitted that her boy seemed more tender of his pet rabbit, as he now knew how delicate the interior organs were.

Most adults have learned to be squeamish, but children naturally welcome any experience that will answer their questions, and anything that tells them about themselves is vitally important. For this reason, after Jean left we continued to use her book. A few older children became adept at dissection. Sometimes they used their skill to help younger ones. For example, a teacher of the five-year-olds arrived one morning to find one of the guinea pigs dead. Of course, the children were upset. They wanted to know why it died, and finally the teacher said she knew some of the sixth graders were very good at dissection; did they want to see the inside of the guinea pig and try to find out why it died? They did.

A note went to the sixth grade asking for a volunteer. Two boys came down, set up a table in the playing yard, told the children only those who wanted to watch were invited, and went to work. Everybody watched. They did a creditable job. They didn't find the cause of death, though they thought it might have been lack of food, for the intestines were empty. There were two embryos, and discovering these thrilled the boys, fascinated the children, and possibly lessened the heaviness of the loss. That there was no food in the digestive tract disturbed them. Even so, it was not as hard as not knowing, and not being able to share the knowledge. It is a mistake to deprive children of a difficult emotional experience. Of such is life, and learning how to meet disturbing situations is best done by sharing them with someone who cares. It was an important experience for the older boys, too; they saw the children in a different light, not just as little nuisances, but as somebodies who needed their knowledge. Their sensitivity came through in answering questions and helping the preschoolers understand how a body works. It was one of those incidental growing-up happenings often missed in our time-hungry world.

When Jean left we found her difficult to replace. Specialists in science are not easy to find, and when found are often not specialists in children. A rapport has to be built up with children, and this is difficult in two science periods a week. No part-time science teacher could be expected to live in the classrooms as Jean did, but that is what every school needs, short of every teacher being competent in science. If children are to develop a scientific attitude, they must carry on long term projects that have nothing to do with 10:30 on Tuesdays and Thursdays, but that are worked on all the time, or at any time.

One of our big projects was to clarify the solar system in the minds of the young. We believed that the idea of the sun and the planets was one of the basic concepts children should feel, think about, act on in their early exploratory period. The sixth grade put up a solar system with the sun outside the science room door. We moved the earth (which was approximately 500 feet distant) in its orbit during the year, from its position by the chicken house in October to a position opposite, in the woods, in April. But these far-reaching arrangements were difficult for children to comprehend. Not being particularly interested in the statistics of distance, they wanted to have the whole thing where they could see it. So our sun and planets began hanging from the ceiling. One eight-year-old decided to have each planet represented by a different size and color of electric light bulb. The planning, framework, and wiring required much help from shop and laboratory, but the group stuck at it and finally had the fun of explaining the finished project to the whole assembly.

34

Another year, my group was occupying a building with windows on four sides; the children put the sun on the ceiling and made a wire orbit for the earth, so it could be moved; other planets were stationary. The windows gave me an idea. I introduced the children to the zodiac, and helped them make these constellations pricked out on black paper and place them in the upper panes of each of the windows, three on a side. It was difficult to think oneself on that earth and sight the sun in the constellation behind it—one way of understanding what was shown by the remark, "You were born when the sun was in Aries." Not all the children got the picture at that point, but at least we played with it.

The concept that the stars are all outside our solar system was hard to come by, but it was demonstrated by sheets with constellations pinned on, placed on walls outside the solar system, and one group managed a tent-like umbrella structure showing both solar system and stars. One teacher, with the children, helped along the idea by placing a tiny solar system at the edge of our woods, and locating Sirius, the nearest star, 400 feet away across the playing field.

There were always new ideas coming up. Mr. Rawson and two boys made a planetarium out of plumbing fixtures, dowels, string, papier mache and an electric light. With this and another very useful piece of apparatus they constructed to show the sun, moon, and earth they could demonstrate an eclipse and the moon's seasons. As with any experience, learning comes from the process; nothing the children ever made looked at all like the beautifully articulated solar system displayed at the planetarium on the parkway in town; but having made their own, they could appreciate the Philadelphia Planetarium and were delighted with the perfection of its solar system and other projections.

Another one of those concepts for children to live with and understand in their bones was the relatedness and interdependence of all forms of life, including those under our very noses on our seven acres, as well as pets brought into the school. Pets were kept for a purpose. The original meaning of the word *science* derives from *scio*, to know; and through pets children begin to know. But they had emotional values, too. Put a guinea pig in the arms of a cranky or frightened child, watch him become whole and serene as he holds it, and you realize that the pet has something to do with his feeling about himself.

Of all the animals that lived with us—rabbits, goats, guinea pigs, hamsters, pigeons, ducks, rats, mice, iguanas, bantams, leghorns, sheep, lambs, bees—the guinea pigs, bantams and bees were the most successful: guinea pigs for their quiet stupidity that allows them to be loved and handled all day long without complaint; bantams for personality differences and their gifts of eggs and chicks; bees for their astonishing exploits both in space and in the hive. Pigeons can have honorable mention for their cooperative family arrangements and for space antics. One group raised carrier pigeons, sending them to be released five, ten, and twenty miles away. We never lost any; they all returned. Another group had a pigeon pen built on the outside of a classroom window, and installed a pair of birds in plain view. These were interesting, for in everything they did, male and female shared the job; father would take over the sitting about noon every day while mother had time off. They never seemed to mind all those eyes on the other side of the glass, even when the young were getting out of the nest. Unfortunately a pair of hawks found out what was going on, and as each tender young pigeon began its first flight, it was swooped up for hawk food.

Bantams very early became attendants at school because of their likeable qualities. The chicken house was near by, and the chickens visited the classrooms by invitation. The chicken house has been built, moved, torn down, rebuilt, given a picture window, reroofed, and patched again and again, and is still an important part of the first grade, cared for by the children. The job of feeding, watering, watching the nests, becomes less drudgery when the first egg appears. That is pure magic, as you can tell when you see the face of the child when he first discovers it. Usually no child has ever met an egg in that situation before. Whoever thought that a breakfast egg was connected with life! But here, this thing came out of a hen! Teacher keeps the eggs carefully so that each child may take one home. Later, the group uses the eggs to make a custard, and, if an old-fashioned freezer can be found, ice cream.

Of course, the most exciting part comes when a hen begins to set. Then twenty-one days are marked on the calendar and plans are made for a wire enclosure for the hen in the classroom during the last few days. Children become two or three degrees quieter, but the hen doesn't mind room noises. If everything goes right, if the eggs are fertile, and if she is secure from rats, the miracle happens and bits of wobbly damp fluff peck their way out of the shells and become chickens. Older children come in, remembering the good feeling of the downy balls of life, and spend some time admiring and petting them.

But it wasn't only reproduction that interested the children. It was the bantams' personality differences that made them especially appealing. They seemed able to learn, and often one of them made noises as if it were talking when it sat on a child's lap. Petey didn't care about petting, being too engrossed in crowing, strutting, and generally being in charge. His trumpet call greeted the first comers each morning, and one Petey (all roosters were "Peteys") followed the janitor around as he unlocked the buildings. It wasn't for food, for that was available; he wanted company. Henny-Penny was a show-off who loved acting. At a play which the older children gave about Audubon and the French settlements on the Ohio, she was one

36

of the important actors and paced back and forth in front of the foot-lights with just the right effect.

The bantams were an important part of our school life. Eloise Holmes and the children in her group had written a book about *Henny and Jenny Penny*. When she died soon afterward, it seemed fitting to make it a memorial to her. Two editions were printed, with pictures hand-colored by parents. It was reviewed by the Horn Book in Boston, and sold to libraries across the country; sixty copies went to New Zealand.

Bees cannot be classified as pets, but perhaps something between a pet and a Western movie, with plenty of mayhem, violence, daring, skills, air stunts, and interpretative dancing. None of this did the children or I get out of our first attempt to raise bees. We started with a lot of the right equipment, but we did not understand what was going on. During the summer, while I was on vacation, the bees weakened and wax moths took over. The result—not only our hives but all the hives in the area had to be destroyed to get rid of the invasion. That failure dampened my enthusiasm for bees for quite some time. Later we tried again, this time with some hives in our woods and an observation hive in one classroom, provided by a friend of the school who offered to keep track of what was happening and explain to us. From that time on, this friend and, later, a bee specialist supervised our hives for several years, during which time the children and I learned to decipher some of what still seems to me an incredible tale. In our first observation hive we had bees without a queen, in the hope that that they were stable enough to make some queen cells while going on with their regular work; we were told to watch carefully to see what happened. Someone saw the first queen emerge, which started the first chapter of mayhem. She found her way to the second queen; whereupon there was a fight and one was killed, we never knew which. But there was no uncertainty about number three—she was smashed before she had a chance to emerge. After that we all knew the queen, though she was difficult to find with the piled-up crowds on top of her and around her as she steadily backed into each prepared cell leaving an egg; 2,000 eggs a day, so the book says. The yellow pollen on the hairy legs of the workers was easy to spot, once we knew what to look for, and to watch as it was deposited in a larva cell. Since a garden was near, we guessed that that was where the pollen came from, and sure enough, there were our bees, busily packing into their leg baskets pollen from the zinnias and asters and chrysanthemums.

One day black and white hornets tried to force their way into the honey, which resulted in a battle worth watching: the guards, helped by cell-cleaners, nurses, undertakers, and foragers joined to outwit the hornets. They succeeded, but it took a long time. Then one fall day the bee specialist happened in when the bees from a hive in the woods were killing their drones. Bee efficiency does not allow winter feeding of these nonworkers; so, after the mating flight they go to work killing the boys. There is no drama, since the drones are defenseless; it is just workers getting rid of waste matter.

As for the dance, it is a kind of ecstatic wiggle that the bee, coming in from a nectar source, indulges in while he makes his way around the comb in the pattern of a figure eight. By the angle of that figure he says something about distance to those whom he is directing. You don't believe it, but there it is.

Though fun was expected, keeping pets was always something besides entertainment for us. A respect for life and the importance of each part in the chain of which we are a link can come from getting intelligently familiar with an animal and taking some responsibility for its welfare.

As an ungraded science project, one spring we set up an experimental program we called *Crosscut*, to give the children an opportunity to select something they wanted to do from an array of choices. We hoped that such a program, set for one-and-one-half-hour periods and cutting across several age groups, would stimulate self-initiated activity. The subject choices offered were science-art, drama-dance, global geography, shop, and finally "undecided." Grades involved were third, fourth, and fifth. Subjects were chosen for a four-week period, at which time the children selected again for a similar period. Here is the June report of the science-art division:

Science-art in the first four weeks tried to discover things about the wind. The children experimented with fans, balloons, vacuums, warm air currents, bellows, musical instruments, wind wheels, sand dunes, sail boats, and ended with some kite-making and some large ceramic masks of wind gods. The teachers selected this focus.

The second group in science-art discussed what they might want to do. Someone suggested making a human heart. In a few minutes it had grown to all the functions. Thus Me-Ho, the Magnificent, the papier mache cadaver on the half shell, was born. The children studied pictures of the viscera and figured out materials to produce them: larynx from Scott foam; esophagus and windpipe from plastic tubing; gall bladder from ceramics; appendix, liver and testicles from Scott foam; blood vessel systems from bell wire; brain from wax. The third graders learned about the functioning of the various organs from the fifth graders who had studied anatomy in their science class. . . .

This type of project, suggested and brought to completion by children, with the teacher as adviser and consultant, shows that facts learned have really become part of them and have been used in a thoughtful and creative fashion.

Our basic goal in science was to get acquainted with the natural forms of life around us, as well as with ourselves, and in that process to find our relationship with other forms. Since attitudes on relationships derived principally from the home, we valued school and home co-operation.

6

APPROACHES TO READING

SINCE A FEW CHILDREN always have difficulty in learning to read, progressive educators early began to make studies of reading readiness. Several schools postponed the beginning of a reading program, recognizing that a common cause of reading failure was immaturity. Since the delayed start seemed sensible, we wanted to try it, but in the first five years, when we were living sometimes from month to month, postponement didn't seem advisable, for we couldn't promise to see our children through to independence. However, in 1935, when we were assured of at least a few years of continuity, we postponed the introduction of the reading program so that it began with our seven-year-olds.

In a *Parents' Bulletin* we reported on all the reading readiness studies we could find, summarized objections we had found to the delay in reading, and gave what we believed to be the likely gains. One objection was that a well-rounded curriculum was difficult without reading. But that was not insurmountable. It was always difficult to get teachers with a full enough living experience of their own to insure rich backgrounds for the children, but we tried. Another objection was that children miss much by not reading. The answer to this was that what they miss is not permanent; the books for younger children are better read aloud anyway, and we did much of this from the nursery years on. A precocious child who starts reading before he has a chance at first-hand experiences and their expression in spoken language can easily retire into books and look for his absorbing pleasure in vicarious experience, a fantasy world unrelated to his life. This is a disservice to him; adults may delight in his prowess, but sooner or later he will have to make up for what he has lost in integrated growth.

39

Another hurdle derived from the current thinking that the sooner a child gets into books the better. Rose Valley parents who had been studying child development questioned this, and were willing to try the delayed attack on reading; but prospective applicants often turned us down, unwilling to take the risk. The reason was obvious. Traditionally, reading was the only criterion by which parents could judge whether their child was "normal." They had waited during the early years, paying some heed to physical and creative accomplishments, but not much, because the only thing that mattered was, "Is he going to pass?"—and that depended largely on his reading. This was understandable when learning was viewed mainly as memorizing the written word. But we believed that the child's reading would be more rewarding if he started later. We urged the acceptance of our new plan and we were heartened when, at about this time, an oculist in Philadelphia heard of our delayed reading plan and sent his approval. He said that children should not have to work with book-sized print before the muscles for fine adjustment of the eyes had developed, which he said occurred around the age of seven.

What this curriculum change meant was that there was more time before the age of seven for creative experience, exploring, and developing motor skills, and incorporating these developments in the languages of play and speech. With this in mind, two of us took a group of fifteen six- and seven-year-olds. We scoured quarries. We walked Ridley Creek each week, starting each time where we had left off the week before, until we reached the source, and the river. We made maps, cooked, worked in shop, in music and in art, getting an understanding of what was around us and building a vocabulary through drama and discussion.

The six-year-olds were encouraged to listen for sounds in spoken words—beginning consonants and rhymes—but the acquaintance with printed words at seven was at first entirely through recognition of their visual patterns. In our program for the six-year-olds we used mathematics rather than reading as the starting point of academic work, for the concrete approach with this was natural and related to the manipulation of tools in shop, laboratory, and kitchen.

Reading material for the seven-year-olds started with labeling objects in the room and dictation from the children about daily happenings. This latter was printed on large wall charts and sometimes illustrated by a child. In modern parlance it was the "language experience" approach.

No effort was made to eliminate big words; if Jimmy's story was about a grasshopper, he was pleased with his big word and that kept it in use. When one-half of the room became a prehistoric forest, *dinosaur* was a favorite word, for several wire and papier-mâché reptiles stalked this forest, making the word important. This reading start was followed later by phonic analyses, including more exercises in rhyming; by the making of picture dictionaries; by recognizing matching words; and in other preliminaries to independent reading. After using wall charts, with primer story content to be cut up and put together, the children were introduced to primers and first readers that had hitherto been kept on a high shelf; after that the going was fast for most of the children. Several basal reading series were used, but seldom beyond the first or second readers. We did not often refer to their "teacher guides," since the activities suggested there were unreal for our pupils. Soon the youngsters were choosing books from our school library. The librarian was also our reading specialist and helped to fit each child's ability and interests to the books we had.

In modern terminology, "language experience," "sight recognition with phonic word-attack skills," and "individualized reading" were the successive steps followed by each child during these years.

During this period the seven-year-olds were seldom advanced two years at the end of one year of reading, but their eagerness was great. They had usually caught up to their age-grade by the end of the second year, and were way ahead after that as their reading skills rapidly approached the grade levels appropriate to their tested "mental ages." When a child had to transfer to another school at six or seven, we worried at first because he had "had so little reading." But after the first few weeks the message usually came from the new teacher, "Send us more like this. The eagerness to learn is remarkable." We, too, felt that eagerness, and we continued the postponed reading plan for it seemed sensible and because the achievement scores of these children in the fourth grade were as high in reading as those who had begun at six, and who were at roughly the same level of intellectual maturity.

However, teachers had been learning too, and by 1947 we felt it no longer necessary to be arbitrary about a beginning reading age. Now we could teach reading to those who were ready at six without making the unready pupils face failure. We had many standards of academic success; reading was not the only criterion.

But not all reading problems were solved by teaching at the right time. Studies of reading and spelling failures, made elsewhere in the late twenties, identified a specific language disability in some children. These were not intellectually inferior boys and girls; they were often gifted.

Sherwood Norman, our teacher of the ten- and eleven-year-olds in 1935, recognized the problem. He suggested that one of our boys be referred to Dr. Orton, a neuropsychiatrist. Later, Margaret Rawson, as our librarian and tutor of this boy according to Dr. Orton's prescription, became very much interested in Orton's approach to teaching children with language learning problems. She

41

studied his theories, as well as those of a wide variety of other reading experts. An article in one of our *Parents' Bulletins* described the nature of the disability as we saw it then:

Dr. Samuel Orton, an American neurologist, beginning in 1925, proposed a hypothesis that reversals, mirror writing, and reading and spelling difficulties result from a failure to develop a distinct dominance (for language) of one cerebral hemisphere over the other. He postulates that the image of the word is stored in one hemisphere, and in the other hemisphere a mirror image is (or may be) stored, and so those individuals who have not developed a dominance of one hemisphere over the other may occasionally recall words or letters which are the mirror images of the original impression. Hence the delay and confusion in learning to recognize words. This hypothesis does not intimate any deficiency of the brain, or necessarily refer to left-handedness, but ambidexterity does seem to occur more often in families with language disabilities. Teaching methods must be designed to impress or repress visual, auditory and kinesthetic memories of sounds, syllables and words upon the dominant hemisphere so that these records will be vivid.

And so the School in Rose Valley started a careful, school-wide testing for language-learning problems and their individualized remedial teaching.[1]

This Orton point of view, Margaret Rawson tells me, has evolved into more sophisticated complexity. Recognized in those days by Orton himself to be partly hypothetical, it is today being increasingly substantiated. On an empirical basis, it enabled her in the thirties at the School in Rose Valley to tutor successfully what are now often called dyslexic children.

Her *Developmental Language Disability; Adult Accomplishments of Dyslexic Boys* is a longitudinal study of fifty-six boys in our school, both dyslexic and non-dyslexic. It refutes the old assumption that dyslexic students are necessarily incapable of performing well in areas requiring language ability. Twenty to thirty years after she had known these boys she renewed her acquaintance with them and in this book reported on their achievements. She compared the twenty in the lowest language-learning facility classifications with twenty at the upper end of her scale. The results showed that the dyslexic boys were not poor academic or occupational risks; they were capable of achievement up to the expectations of their intelligence and family educational and occupational patterns, even when these were at the highest professional levels. In fact, they scored a bit above their schoolmates who had found language skills easy to learn. This book shows that this disability need not be an insuperable handicap.

[1] See Margaret Rawson, *Developmental Language Disability* (Baltimore: The Johns Hopkins Press, 1968).

The sight method approach to reading, supplemented by analytic phonics, with individualized special tutoring for serious problems, described our reading program for a considerable period. However, in 1961 Bloomfield and Barnhart's *Let's Read*[2] was published, giving the story of a linguist's approach to reading. The linguist, Leonard Bloomfield, had evolved the system to teach his own boys. He said that schools were teaching reading as if our English writing were made up of ideographs instead of letters, when, in fact, our writing is based on an alphabet. Children learned words by memorizing their configurations, but that did not, in itself, give them a means to attack new words. With good visual memories children could learn enough sight words to begin, and analytic phonics came along to make them independent readers. This wasn't the most efficient way to learn to read an alphabetically recorded language, said the linguists. Since our English spelling (or writing) is based on twenty-six letters, the reasonable approach is to learn what these look like and their names, and then to proceed to learn that letters represent sounds within words. This is begun by learning three letter words with short vowel sounds—man, pan, ban, etc. Almost at once the child knows mad, pad, bad, and so on to mat, pat, bat, and the decoding process is begun.

I gave the book to the first grade teacher, Jo Faulkner, who liked new ideas, saying, "This turns upside down an old notion of ours, that children should begin with 'interest' words, taken from experience; *man, pan, ban* are certainly not interest words, but this approach makes another kind of sense. Let's try it." She was willing, and in February 1962 began trying it out. Almost at once the children were caught. The interest was not in meaning, primarily, though the importance of getting meaning was not lost sight of, but in the fact that here was a *key* they could use to decode and encode words they already knew and others, too. Since regularly sounded and spelled words form from sixty to seventy per cent of our language, the children rapidly acquired a considerable reading vocabulary.

At this time we discovered that in Miquon, a school similar to ours north of Philadelphia, Lynn Goldberg, the first grade teacher, and Donald Rasmussen, principal of the school, had started to use the linguistic method the previous year. They were now organizing a group of co-operating schools to work with them and Science Research Associates of Chicago[3] to produce test materials, workbooks, games, stories, and methods of introducing the linguistic materials

[2] L. Bloomfield and C. Barnhart, *Lets Read* (Wayne State University Press, 1961).

[3] D. Rasmussen and L. Goldberg, *Basic Reading Series* (Science Research Associates, 1965).

for classroom use. We joined the group, and a workshop in which we met and shared experiences with teachers from different kinds of schools in Boston, Washington, and Philadelphia. We continued (and the school still continues) to use Miquon's material. This approach to reading combines the best of the sight and phonics methods with linguistic facts and principles about spelling. It appeals to children, partly because it allows independent work in unlocking spelling patterns. In one year and one-half the children learn to decode all the common spelling patterns in our language, and they can use this method as a tool for expressing their ideas. Here is a sample of a group recipe composed by a second grade:

BIM BAM HOT POT

Get a big pot
Put a bit of wet mud in it
Lug in a big fat hog
And cut it up and put it in the pot
Get ten big fat hens
Put them in
Put in one big cup of wax
And a lot of eggs
Put in a big can of gas
Put the top on the pot
Run to the big pit
Do not lag or you will be hit
Sit in the pit and hum a bit
As the pot gets hot
Bim bam bim bam bim bam BOOM
Get a cab or a bus and a big map
Go to Sam's or Max's to eat.

We were satisfied that these authors were making good progress in reading (or decoding), and in understanding content.

7

LANGUAGE

J UDGED BY THE STANDARDS of schools where teachers do the talking and the children keep still, our children talked too much; but we adhered to a philosophy of "learning by doing," and thus we encouraged the pupils to speak freely. Language, being a means of communication, has to be acquired in a social atmosphere. We thought continually about the process of learning and were entirely in agreement with Harold Taylor's interesting ideas:[1]

Everything educates and some things more than others. Springtime educates, for example. So do sunsets, winters, poems, the ocean, plays, books, sounds, situations, people, and in the last analysis raw experience.

The direction of learning is from emotion to thought to expression in words, symbols, or symbolic action of some kind—not the reverse, as most educators think. Educators think that by exposure to symbols, words, and connected concepts, thoughts will be formed and children will become educated; they will be able to read, write and speak what they have learned. Education should, then, be formal, academic and confined to the classroom.

This puts the matter backward, of course, but the educational system keeps going along backward and its critics keep attacking for the wrong reasons. They can't attack it for going backward, but for not being backward enough, not giving children more symbols, more words, concepts and facts in a shorter time.

Emotion, then, is the starting point of the learning process; the child must be involved if he is to get meaning and understanding. We found that discussion periods after something had happened, or during an experiment, were bound to be lively; if they weren't,

[1] *Saturday Review*, May, 1963.

something was the matter. Anyone can learn by rote that three fives are fifteen and that air has pressure, but he won't know what these facts *mean* without asking questions, doing something, talking about what he did, and about why he did it.

Children at Rose Valley have always been encouraged to talk about what they do and how they feel while the experiences are fresh; to listen to others, children and adults; to be read to and to read; to dictate and to write.

The kind of questions a child asks, the kind of experimentation he engages in during his early years, determine the kind of questions he will continue to ask when he enters books. One conventional school pattern we were trying to change was the attitude that everything in books is sacred. Books were open to questions, as were all activities. Not that we aimed to be constant or destructive critics, but to be alert to words and thoughtful of their meaning.

That is what all the talking meant. The School in Rose Valley is organized to encourage communication among parents, teachers, and children. Each group has its own organization and areas of work, and each needs contact with the others for understanding and being understood. We urged parents to visit this school, and others; teachers were expected to visit the homes of their pupils; apprentice teachers had a weekly discussion period, as did the regular teachers.

The children had many kinds of discussion sessions. The assemblies, general meetings, and class meetings were planned so that from the early years children could practice speaking in public and could find out what it meant to hold audience interest, to organize material for presentation, and to answer questions. On Wednesdays the preschool had its assembly, sometimes attended by older children; on Fridays the whole school met in an assembly arranged and managed by each of the grades in turn. In the older groups, children learned parliamentary procedure—how to chair a meeting, to carry through a vote, to recognize differing points of view. They learned to hunt for solutions to perplexing problems, and to deal with failure constructively.

In all of this the child had to do his own thinking. He had to defend his own position, listen to others, refute reasonably, clear up misconceptions, draw conclusions. Therefore, it was important to speak clearly, hold the discussion to the point, base arguments on facts, and to "say what you mean, and stop when you have said it." In written language similar skills were encouraged. The monthly magazine *Leaves*, and later the weekly newspaper, gave children practice in learning to express, communicate, describe, report, criticize, and explain.

Schools used to begin at the wrong end in teaching language: grammar and punctuation first, writing second; just as at one time the child in shop had to saw straight lines and hammer straight

46

nails before he was allowed to make anything. This was before we were concerned with the *process* of learning. From the beginning at Rose Valley we realized the importance of discovery. We let the children write and build from the very start and helped them both with grammar and with the manipulation of saws and hammers. Both pupils and teachers sensed the thrill and the importance of the first creative efforts.

There were many ways to supplement language study. Sherwood Norman, teaching ten- and eleven-year-olds, exposed them to propaganda analysis; this led to collecting examples of propaganda devices (name-calling, glittering generalities, band wagon, etc.); to the study of newspapers, comparing front pages, advertisements, visiting the *Chester Times*, and to analyzing their own magazine for propaganda. Pat Beatts, teacher of the twelve- and thirteen-year-olds, used Hayakawa's *Language in Action*[2] as a way into the study of the why and how of words, and what they do *to* you as well as *for* you. He found that work in logic, rational thinking, classifications, generalizations, etc. had been valuable in improving written and verbal expression, and in countering emotionalism.

Mathematics is a language too. Pat Beatts, realizing the inadequacy of our math texts, worked out with Margaret Rawson a rational approach to math which emphasized understanding of meaning (a precursor of the "new math"). In later years, Peg Nowell continued our work on meaning, teaching some algebra and geometry to the older children and helping teachers with mathematical thinking. In 1949, when Catherine Stern's *Children Discover Arithmetic*[3] was published, we made in shop ten sets of the material described in her book (blocks, cubes, and a pattern board), and invited her to visit the school. Her materials and her talk helped us immeasurably with mathematical language. Years later, a two-year staff study of the new mathematics with Dan Goldwater, a Swarthmore mathematician, put us further along and increased both the children's and the adults' understanding of mathematical symbols.

Probably nothing the teachers ever did helped language practices as much as a class in poetry writing they organized for themselves and kept going for two years, with Alexandra Docili, an artist from Pendle Hill (a Quaker Retreat and Study Center in Wallingford, Pennsylvania). She had everybody writing and liking it; and—more interesting—teachers noted how much the children's writing improved. (See chapter 10.)

Then, at an opportune moment for us to open a new approach to language, came *People in Quandries*, a book on semantics by Wendell Johnson.[4] Johnson showed that the language of people in

[2] S. Hayakawa, *Language In Action* (2nd ed.; Harcourt, Brace, 1964).
[3] Catherine Stern, *Children Discover Arithmetic* (Harper, 1949).
[4] Wendell Johnson, *People in Quandries* (Harper, 1946).

quandries consitutes in large measure the very stuff their quandries are made of. The whole book was fascinating for many adults; it was another introduction to semantics that changed our thinking.

In all of this work with language, it is obvious that we have been concerned only with our own tongue, and can be criticized justly for having taught a foreign language during only one-third of the school's history: German for the first three years, and French for the last ten. But Margaret Mead, when she talked to our parents and teachers on "Basic Anthropological Ideas for Children," assured us of an even greater need than studying foreign languages; the need to teach our children that *our* culture is not *the* culture; that man is a species, no matter what the size, shape or color of its representatives, and related to the natural world; that humans are one kind of creature, all having essentially the same physical and mental equipment; that no special people are carriers of progress. That is, if we want to save ourselves we must save all mankind, even our enemies. Our language is just one of many languages and learning another one helps make this attitude our own.

The language we use determines to some extent the way we think. We worked for free and open talk, for tolerance and for self understanding, and for as much understanding of other people as we could acquire. In working toward these goals our library was very important.

We started collecting children's books of other countries partly because we felt strongly that we needed the world brought into our small provincial corner, and partly because some of the best books published in the thirties came from foreign countries. Since we were in a rural area, we needed a good natural science library; and since children are naturally poets and artists, we sought out good poetry and art. Luckily, Ann Pennell, a school founder, incorporator, and guiding spirit, was a book collector, and soon after the school was started, she opened BOOKWAYS, a book shop in Rose Valley and later in Swarthmore. She gave the school library its first 350 books, got many others for us at cost, and used our librarian to try out her newest acquisitions for genuine reactions from children. At Christmas time she displayed at the school the best of each year's books for children, sold them to parents, and gave the profits to our library. We gathered many excellent books (some in translations) about children in other countries. Outstanding was a collection of about 75 German picture books, the gift of another incorporator, Irmgard Taylor, who was our German teacher for three years.

Building a library to 4,000 volumes on a budget of fifty dollars a year was no mean accomplishment. The annual library budget gradually increased to one hundred dollars, and only thirty-five years later did it reach eight hundred dollars. Individual donations of cash or books helped considerably. Our librarian spent long hours

48

at LEARY'S, a second-hand bookstore in Philadelphia, picking up three dollar books for thirty cents. She collected and filed pictures, magazine articles, and pamphlets to supplement our reference library. Sometimes she gathered source material from Philadelphia, Swarthmore, and local public libraries. The job of librarian was on a tuition-exchange basis, and often a mother started as librarian when her child entered and stayed until the youngest of her family had graduated; hence she had time to get acquainted with the books and the children, and to become a stable presence so necessary in a well-used library. Our librarians did a major job in whetting children's appetites and matching books to their interests so that the library was a well-loved room and reading was a favorite occupation. The children felt that it was theirs and were disarmingly frank in offering criticisms and suggestions. When they visited another school where there was no rest period after lunch, the first question was, "When do they have time to read?"

The library was a place always in need of volunteer help. Sometimes a child would coax his mother, "Why don't you work at school?" Library work was one of the jobs on the list given incoming parents to encourage them to become involved. Another service the library offered parents was the adult bookshelf in the office. When they asked for something to read on education, or a particular problem, we gave them books such as: *Education Through Art*, by Herbert Read; *New Ways in Discipline*, by Dorothy Baruch; *The Process of Education*, by Jerome Bruner; *The Aims of Education*, by Alfred North Whitehead; *Emotional Maturity*, by Leon Saul (our friend and consultant); and *Perceiving, Behaving, Becoming: A New Focus in Education.*[5]

Every year the staff discussed new books on education, and in 1963 we were particularly stimulated by Sylvia Ashton-Warner's *Teacher.*[6] Her interest in Tolstoy's school started us hunting and reading everything Tolstoy had written on education, with the result that two parent-teachers, Lee Stephens and Ann Rawson, edited a paperback book *Leo Tolstoy on Education*, dedicated to Sylvia Ashton-Warner, and in 1964 had 200 copies printed by the Roberts Press in Media. This printing was quickly sold, and we understand that in 1967 the University of Chicago Press published a similar book which we can recommend.[7]

---

[5] Read (Pantheon, 1958); Baruch (McGraw, 1949); Bruner (Harvard University Press, 1960); Whitehead (Macmillian, 1929); Saul (Lippincott, 1947); *Perceiving, Behaving, Becoming* (National Education Association Yearbook, 1962).

[6] Simon & Schuster, 1963.

[7] *Tolstoi on Education*, edited by Reginald D. Archambault (University of Chicago Press, 1967).

8

SOCIAL STUDIES

O UR SOCIAL STUDIES had two main objectives. The first was to learn everyday methods of democratic living. The second was to get an idea of the sweep of history from the beginning of life to the present.

For the first, we had to identify areas in which the children would have real responsibilities, and we had to set aside time in the curriculum for meetings of the children and their teachers in which organization and management to meet these responsibilities were worked out.

We felt that unless children had daily experience in adjusting to change and in understanding and working with individuals of different temperaments the lessons of history and of current events would not seem related. In that case, these future citizens would fumble, as so often do their elders. The ten- and eleven-year-olds, for example, had a class organization run by parliamentary rules, and everyone took turns conducting the meetings. Of course, some problems could not wait for a formal meeting and these were settled on the spot, usually by the children. I early learned that a child's direct approach and simple common sense can solve a surprising number of problems, and I tried to harness my own impulse to interfere. The chore-board in each room showed regular weekly job assignments: room managing, cleaning lunch trays, sweeping, cleaning sink, straightening library shelves. The irregular jobs, such as membership on committees on assemblies, games, general meetings, grounds, *Leaves* (the school magazine), and plays, all lasted for the time necessary to finish the job. The annual camping trips, lasting from three days to a week, had to be planned, menus made, supplies bought, meals cooked, and cleaning up done.

This understanding of different temperaments and having to live with all of them was the most important means of learning, for we sometimes took in disturbed children who did their bit in upsetting the groups. Many staff discussions were spent in deciding whether we would take so-and-so, or whether keeping him was in his own interest and that of the group. Groups were small, (enrollment in 1933 was 38; in 1935 it was 55) so there were no more than a dozen children of two or three ages in each class. It would seem that in a small group the unhappy child could easily be assimilated; on the other hand, that child's influence and the damage he might do was proportionately greater than in a large class. We discussed this damage and argued about it, and usually couldn't find it. It didn't hurt a child to see another child's problems; it seemed to contribute to his understanding.

One year we took in a six-year-old who had been expelled from the public school because of his disruptive behavior. He had charm —and a body full of hostility. He was also gifted and, to the children's delight, had wonderful building ideas; he also could produce more dissension than any three others. When the children couldn't cope, I would seat him on a chair and ask him to watch for a while until he felt he could go back to the group without fighting. One time, when I was unusually bothered, I put him in another room to give the children some peace. They came to me, reminding me how much he had improved and said, "Oh Rotzy, give him another chance. He's going to be all right." I did, and he was. I found that this was often the case: children are good at learning how to cope with other children; when they want a child to improve, he usually improves.

A six-year-old in this sort of school gets an honest feeling of competence. When one boy told the group, "You can't do better than have me for a stage manager; I'm very good at it," his egotism was based on fact. He was not an offensive boy. He was competent and knew it, and that was as it should be. He had learned about himself from experience in group activities.

Experience also fosters judgment. A parent told us about a six-year-old who was given money to buy a present for a seven-year-old. He went to a toy store and rejected one toy after another. Finally, a weary salesman said that he had the very thing, and showed him a truck which, wound up, would go until it struck a wall, reverse and go back, reverse and go back until it ran down. The six-year-old said, "It bores *me*, and he is a year older than I am." He ended by buying his friend an emery wheel.

This, then, was the general pattern. The child's learning how to live in a group came from his daily experiences; his understanding of how man lives and has lived through the ages came from subject matter that he must investigate: first, by going and looking—the

51

here and now observations of how man lives (how does he get water, bread, milk, etc.?); and second by going to books, local historians, museums, the planetarium, science institutes, regional librarians. For all ages, the search for the right material was a time-consuming and never-ending task. The following excerpts indicate the subject matter in our first social studies program. Here is a quotation from a curriculum report of the six-year-old group in 1936:

The important things children need to learn at this age are how to think, how to observe, and how to use what they have observed and thought in a constructive way. To supply these needs we have set to work studying our community. We take weekly trips to the post office, to a coal yard, to the river front, to a store, for example, and then during the rest of the week we use these observations in block play. The block period is an hour and a half long. During these periods each child becomes part of the community. The block town now has in it a post office, bank, school, gas station, store, hospital, barber shop, and cemetery. There is a river of blue oilcloth with docks, ferry boats, tugs and liners, and a coal yard on the river front; up in the balcony country (we had a split-level classroom) are a farm, an airport, and a firehouse. Not all of these buildings are made every day. The scene constantly changes. Due to the fact that the room has to be free for other activities, block buildings cannot stay up. Even so, the same person has been postmaster for weeks, the same person has been the farmer, and usually a child keeps an activity going for a period of days. For example, after we had made the train trip from Moylan to Swarthmore, we chalked on the floor the relation of the train tracks to the road and the stores. Then the buildings were put up and lively play resulted. Trucks carried mail, the store delivered goods, the farmer brought pumpkins to the store and the hospital. The hired man stayed home and made box stalls for the horses. The gas station attendants greased cars and sold gasoline. The bank supplied money to the storekeepers.

The morning begins with a discussion period. Here we talk about the needs of the town, how the schoolhouse could be improved, whether the water wheel could be made to run an elevator to the balcony, why the battery that supplied lights for the airport was run down this morning etc. Then activity takes over.

This report shows that this hour and one-half activity period was directed as much to that first aim of social studies—learning to live together—as it was to learning about the environment. For here children were being themselves, with all their hostilities and fears mixed in with creative urges and constructive drives. There were bound to be clashes; but it was amazing to me, in my first year as a teacher of six-year-olds, how quickly they adjusted, how easily they came to sizing up situations and contributing solutions. The teacher probably learned more than the children.

One activity was typically related to another in our curriculum. The first field trip taken by our seven-year-olds one autumn was to the top of the Crozer Building in Chester, Pennsylvania, to get a

52

bird's-eye view of the river. Soon afterward we started to make a model just outside our classroom building. We enlarged a government topographical map of this section. We took other trips to nearby Long Point, to the sewage plant, to Springfield Reservoir; we made Ridley and Crum creeks on our model and located these places. A hose extending from the building furnished water for the creeks and the river. Another activity of the seven-year-olds was to build a model town. This was a group project which had been going on outdoors since March. It was an indirect result of trips we took, but had little specific relation to anything the children had seen. It was an imaginary town, built around a public square in the center of which was a pool. Most of the interest and effort was spent on the pool, rock garden, and road. The houses were painted. The firehouse had a belfry and two trucks; the gas station, two trucks and a tow car; the hospital had the beginning of an elevator. At first only five children worked on the model, but by the end of May all were involved.

The children in our school delved deeper into a problem than might have been expected, and developed longer attention spans. They had more complications to contend with; for example, the addition of water into the model town made planning more difficult —and also more interesting. Everybody's engineering skill was needed. The children learned about a community and about maps; they also learned how to accept each other's ideas, how to let go and when to hold on to their own ideas.

As the children grew older they reached out in their wonder about the far away and long ago. "What was there before there was anything?" Eight- and nine-year-olds have a long reach in their imagination, as well as being still mostly concerned with the here and now. Fortunately, in 1933 Eloise Holmes joined our teaching staff. She also had a long reach; she valued the children's ideas and could draw them out and work happily with them.

And in 1935, just when we needed it most, an unusual book, *The Story of Earth and Sky*, by Carleton Washburne and the teachers of Winnetka, Illinois, was published.[1] It had been started in the science department of the San Francisco State Teachers' College, where it was worked out with children in their training school. Then for ten years Winnetka teachers had used this material, revising it with the children's help, and finally producing this book of sure-fire interest to the young. It has been in constant use over the years, and has been the incentive for many a meaningful project, drama, dance, mural, and star party. One year, in one of Eloise Holmes' classes, a group of eight-year-olds had been working on their

[1] C. Washburne, *The Story of Earth and Sky* (Appleton, 1935).

solar system for a week. Gradually the meaning of *planet* came clear. Jimmy made a model of Jupiter, and after he put it in its proper place, he said, "So that's what we're talking about! Now I catch!"

Our studies of astronomy led into the study of the beginning of life (cells and their development into plants and animals), of dinosaurs, cave man, Indians, and up to recorded history; but never was this covered in one year. In a two-age group a child could spend two years getting an idea of how man came to be and what his life was like in earlier times. And along with the story of ancient times we continued our exploration of the environment, regularly visiting quarries, woods, and streams.

We *made* things relating to our studies, and this was very important. When making a map of the Panama Canal (it was not prehistory, but the children wanted to know about it) the group wanted to understand canal locks. So, in the yard, they made two miniature lakes with a channel—and locks—between. Another group, interested in fossils after reading Roy Chapman Andrews' *On the Trail of Ancient Man*,[2] produced a never-to-be-forgotten play about the Gobi Desert. In fact, that fall their playground *was* the Gobi Desert and digging was a serious pursuit. The eight-year-olds, with Mr. Rawson's help, made a wood-burning kiln and fired their own pottery. They also helped make the incinerator.

The long morning work period was classified as social studies, but had in it something of every subject offered because real living was going on. Eloise Holmes helped immeasurably in the original planning and in getting the school and the children off to a good start. As a teacher she made children feel that they *belonged*, not to her, although they felt close, but to themselves and to the world; they learned to meet it easily and to become part of it.

In 1935, when our oldest group had reached ten and eleven years of age, Sherwood Norman arrived, from the Dalton School in New York, to be their teacher for their last two years in our school. He came at the right time to carry on into research with books the ferment of exploration and discovery of the environment. He understood the preadolescent's urge to be his own teacher, and he made the children, in their sprawling leaning stage feel dignified and independent. For example, each child had an individual monthly work sheet specifying "work to be done this month, when, where, and how you like." Several periods a week were given to this planned individual work. Although the general outline of basic concepts had been agreed upon by the staff, the teacher and children worked out the parts in which they were to be engaged and decided

[2] (Putnam and Sons, 1926.)

how they would work. The first plan included reviewing work of the previous year and connecting it with conditions and events leading up to the first indications of civilized life, then Egypt, Greece, and the Middle Ages. (This was also a two-age group, hence a two-year plan.) The schedule allowed for the time-consuming discussions necessary not only for group living but for the children's understanding of their research. The discussion was also planned to clarify the connection between at least one current event and the children's own lives. Here are excerpts from reports:

We discussed the possibility of making a time line (one million years to the foot was decided upon) to show the relative lengths of the periods of the development of life. We made lists of the ages and approximate number of years between. . . .

When the time line was finally pounded into place, several weeks later along a nine hundred foot lane on the school grounds, the first sign was a clearly painted white board on which was printed:

HERE LIFE BEGAN

about 1,000 million years ago.

This line represents the growth and development of life from the first single cell to man. The line is 1,000 feet long, each foot equals 1,000,000 years. And six signs and a million years later, it ended with the arrival of Man, whose sign was outside the classroom door.

In that same week the situation in Ethiopia was referred to and a discussion period planned. Here is the teacher's report:

A fifteen minute period had been planned. It lasted an hour, with interest keen . . .. A list of topics follows, in order of discussion, each subject being in response to questions raised:

1. Difference between ancient and modern wars.
2. Economic and other causes for war vs. the excuses for war.
3. This led to empire building and how each nation gradually acquired more territory; why one could hold its territory and others not; the extent of Britain's empire and why she is a successful colonizer; Japan and Manchuria.
4. Back again to Italy and Ethiopia. Italy's problem.
5. The League of Nations, what it is and why the U.S. is not a member; whether she could really stay out of a world struggle if she wanted to; the interdependence of nations; how money or goods get tied up; war debts. Back to the League and sanctions—what they mean, what will happen next week if sanctions are brought against Italy; Why England and France are concerned; the Nile.
6. And last of all—law vs. war, and how it has worked through the ages: family, tribe, clan, state, nation, world . . ..

Fortunately most of these children came from families where discussions like this were common; but, if they had not come from a background of this sort we would have felt it our responsibility to start such thinking. This is the stage of development where very pertinent questions are being asked and they need honest answers, or honest admission of ignorance or confusion, as an incentive to learning and thinking.

Sherwood Norman's enthusiasm for learning caught the children, and they responded to his expectation of their independence. He was careful to give them ways of being on their own. This sometimes led into unexpected social problems, as happened in the course of producing a play.

Everyone was wrapped up in the story of Joseph, a play taken directly from the Old Testament, and they were working very hard indeed, each child composing his part as he acted, and changing it to fit the criticism of the group. The large number of characters involved necessitated several children's taking two or three parts; there were to be six sets of scenery; costumes, using Egyptian designs, required considerable experimenting; and the property committee was busy making an Egyptian oven, a throne, a carrying-chair, a water skin, fans, and spears. Because of illness there had been many absences, but now work on the play was resumed.

All went well until Tuesday when Polly became ill and failed to return. This meant that the parts of the Chief Baker, Street Seller and Benjamin had to be filled by someone else. Sylvia, who already knew her part of the Story Teller, volunteered and did one scene beautifully. She could take over for Polly. The play must go on!

Our first obstacle seemed on the way to solution when another followed. Luncheon periods had grown rather disorderly. Tuesday's was impossible. Words having no effect whatever, I simply got up and left the room, determined not to come back until the children realized the need for a teacher and asked me to return. I didn't return until the afternoon of the following day. In the meantime there followed a most interesting example of group psychology.

The entire class determined to carry on without me. Lunch dishes were returned, rest (a silent reading period) was carried on as usual for an hour, with ten minutes extra. The afternoon was spent working on costumes, much as though I had been present except that during recess everything possible was done to get my attention, such as parading through the empty room where I was busy dyeing curtains for the play, etc. The next morning, realizing that I was not going to help them, they determined to give the play without my help. The date was set a week ahead and the poster in the hall changed. Then followed such activity as was never seen before! What parts needed to be rehearsed most? What scenery was finished? What not? We must train the Chipsters (eights and nines taking minor parts); "shine up" Sylvia for Benjamin, Chief Baker and Street Seller . . . and so on. A list of things to be done was put on the blackboard. The office pointed out to the children that the play couldn't be postponed because it had been announced for this Friday. So the date was changed back again, and even more feverish activity ensued.

Several times during the morning I was found in the library, or observing in another classroom, and asked a question, but the answer was always, "This is your problem if you don't need a teacher." One time when Bobby's fooling made it impossible to rehearse, and they had appealed to me without avail, I found him banished to the library, doing arithmetic. Observers recorded everybody feverishly busy. Even shop and dancing—their favorite special subjects—were discarded because they "had no time." Parts were rehearsed, and gone over again as criticisms were made. They were determined to carry through at all costs to show up Sherwood Norman. After lunch on Wednesday Grace decided to talk it over with them. She discovered that they had never once allowed themselves to think that they had been at fault, but rather I was at fault for having dared to leave them like that—and just before a play, too! Grace asked Scotty what he would have done had he been the teacher. She pointed out the responsibility of the play, and asked them if they could do it without help; she left it to them to decide whether they might at least offer to talk it over with me—an idea that had not entered their heads.

Ten minutes later a chorus was heard in the hall: "Let bygones be bygones and forget the past." When asked if this meant they wanted me back, they said yes, and agreed to alter conditions at lunch and consider my feelings as a person as well as the leader of their group.

One could almost see the relaxation as the responsibility was lifted from their shoulders. Yet the value of this experience in self-direction, which far overshadowed any lessons that might be learned from the original issue, also overshadowed any possible harm from the physical and emotional tension evidenced those days. There is no doubt they were immensely pleased with the work they had accomplished all by themselves.

With two obstacles overcome, the third greeted us the next morning. Norman, the student who took the part of Joseph, had symptoms of flu and had to remain at home. No one but Sylvia would volunteer even to try the long part. To postpone the play again was impossible. The day was spent in one dress rehearsal of each scene, with plenty of rest in between. It was the only time all the scenes were put together. Sylvia proved she could handle the role of Joseph as well as her original part of the Story Teller. She remembered Norman's role almost word for word. Towny was trained as Benjamin, and I filled in as Chief Baker and Street Seller. Those who had to change costumes between scenes trained another child to assist them, so that my only activity next morning besides minor parts, was to help draw the curtain and change scenery. The play, lasting over an hour, went off successfully Friday morning.

Here was another teacher who helped lay the foundation of a school where people wanted to learn; he could help children succeed and fail (both valuable experiences), and succeed again, in the daily problems of living. Without marks or prizes of any kind he made learning exciting; though he never required homework, the children often did it of their own accord. One of this group said later, when he had entered seventh grade in another school, "I am busier this year, but not working as hard." As an adult he was to say, "One of the most important values I developed in The School in Rose Valley was that one can confidently approach jobs with the assumption that they will be interesting."

This plan for social studies, worked out by the early teachers in the school, was always considered subject to the interests of both teachers and children. As people have changed, there has been variation. The goal has been to explore deeply rather than to cover broadly, and whenever children have spent long times in the Gobi Desert, or in space, or at the bottom of the ocean, or just finding their way, no matter how wasteful it seemed to some, we felt that the time was well spent in learning how to learn, and in depth of personal and social experience.

9

A VIEW OF SOCIAL STUDIES

PEG NOWELL*

DURING THE YEARS in which I taught the oldest group (ages ten and eleven), social studies came to be our favorite subject because, as the children put it, "There's so much to find out about, and so many different things to do."

Over each two-year span we worked within the school's concept of "the flow of history," trying to get a feeling of the past and to orient ourselves, both chronologically and geographically. One year we studied man from prehistoric times through the early civilizations and on into the Middle Ages. The second year we started with the early explorers of our own world and ended with the then embryonic journeys into outer space. It did not seem to matter to an incoming fifth grade which of these experiences came first; there were values in relating the present to the past, as well as the past to the present.

Within this general plan there was great flexibility so that the desires and interests of the students could be followed. One year we

---

* In the following pages Peg Nowell, teacher of the group of fifth and sixth graders from 1947 to 1964, writes of social studies, creative writing, and the making of plays during those later years.

Peg held a variety of positions in the school before she began to teach. Entering in 1933 as a tuition-exchange parent, she worked first as an assistant with the four- and five-year-old group, then with the six-year-olds. She then became secretary and assistant treasurer of the school and managed the office with a sense of humor and great understanding of the human ego. In an emergency, when I took the group of twelve- and thirteen-year-olds, I asked her to be the assistant, for I believed she was ready to teach. She was. After two years as an assistant she taught the oldest group (fifth and sixth grades were from then on the oldest group in the school) until her retirement in 1964. She was one of those rare teachers who is gratefully remembered.

might cover briefly many former civilizations—Sumaria, Egypt, Crete, China, India, the Hebrews, Greece and Rome. Another group might choose to spend a whole semester studying Egypt or Greece or England during the Middle Ages, or might become interested in comparative religions as a continuing theme throughout the year. This held true, also, when studying the New World. Sometimes we included Canada, Mexico, and the countries of South America; other years the children wanted "straight" United States history, or asked for a long block of time on such special subjects as the American Revolution, the Westward Migration, or the causes of the Civil War.

One September, two sixth grade girls who had studied the New World the previous year, announced that they did not want to learn about older civilizations; they felt that this would be a waste of time since there was so much they didn't know about the modern world. Others disagreed, and sides were chosen for a formal debate. The speakers prepared for this seriously, and the arguments were both lively and thought-provoking. After the debate, the class voted for studying the past, but certainly with an improved understanding of "the uses of history." The losing side accepted defeat gracefully and enjoyed the year's work once it was under way. Of course, as was always true, we spent lots of time investigating and discussing current happenings.

I was not imaginative enough that year to figure out a possible compromise, but later I did experiment with some comparative history. While some children reported on Columbus and Magellan, others told about the first astronauts. When the majority were studying the American Revolution, three small groups found out about the French, Russian, and Chinese revolutions and reported on these. Individual research enabled us to compare the problems of the newly independent African countries with the difficult early years of our own republic, and to discuss the effect on people's lives of different types of government. The most mature students found this approach fascinating, but for many it was confusing and hard to understand. Perhaps this challenging way of learning history belongs at an older age level.

Whatever subject we were about to investigate, the start was always a group discussion, or a series of discussions. What do we already know? What would we like to find out? Is it really worth studying at all? The teacher had already placed around a few pictures and artifacts, chosen for their question-raising value. A list, in bold black printing, of strange new words such as "ankh," "dynasty," "shaduf," "acropolis," etc. was sure to arouse curiosity and a rush for dictionaries.

After our discussions, the children were turned loose to read on their own about the country or the period we were entering. We had in our room a variety of reference books, relevant fiction, and, of course, encyclopedias. There might be three or four copies of the best-liked textbooks, but never a "set" from which everyone studied. It was not always easy to find material for all of the reading levels represented. Most of the children could cope quite well with material written for adults. The less competent readers objected strongly to being talked down to by authors ("Now we will get into Uncle Ben's big airplane and fly over the great, sandy Sahara desert"). I wrote many letters to publishers protesting this sort of writing in social studies textbooks; others must have made similar criticisms for, gradually, better books began to appear. The most popular textbook in the room was written for high school students. As we started each new subject, our school librarian added to our shelves books from the local public libraries and other sources.

After a few periods of general background reading (with frequent interruptions to share exciting bits of information), we talked about writing reports. A blackboard list was made of the things we wanted to find out about: houses, clothing, customs, food, schools, government, religion, amusements, sports, important people and events— whatever anyone wanted to know. Sometimes each child chose one of these topics; sometimes a small group worked together on a report. Two students might do separate reports on the same subject if they wished; their different points of view often made this interesting, as did the occasional, important discovery that their reference sources did not always agree with respect to facts. We worked on taking notes and making outlines, and this was useful in producing clear, well-constructed reports.

Because few children wanted to spend all of each social studies period writing reports, other things were soon under way simultaneously. Time lines continued to be a favorite project. These might be simple linear projections to scale, or balls of yarn—each civilization a different color and length—which the makers unwound and explained in assembly, delighted with the surprise of the younger children when the United States proved to be the last, tiny red-white-and-blue inch of yarn. But the picture time lines were the most fun for everyone. Each child painted (with poster paint on a 12" by 18" piece of cardboard) one or more pictures about each period or civilization we studied. The completed pictures were given titles and dates and put up around the walls in chronological sequence; they added color and excitement to the classroom, and also enabled the children to see quickly and easily the order in which events occurred. One ten-year-old, returning to Rose Valley after five years in another school, followed the time line around the room with interest, and then remarked, "Why, I thought the Pilgrims were the beginning of history!"

Other activities that went on during social studies periods included

A classroom

the making of three-dimensional scenes on a long, broad shelf built for this purpose. The most ambitious of these was a representation of a block in the Philadelphia of 1776. We made a trip to sketch details of Independence Hall and the houses in Elfreth's Alley (a Colonial restoration). In shop, supervised by an expert carpenter, a group of fifth grade boys made models of all the buildings. The girls painted a backdrop (which included the duckpond where City Hall now stands) and the buildings, taking great care to get a "real brick red" for the latter. Two boys patiently drew bricks on the red buildings with rulers and white pencils; others fashioned tiny, swinging signs for the shops and the inn, and miniature trees for Independence Square, paved cobblestoned Market Street with pebbles, and glued in place the dials from four toy watches to make the clock on Independence Hall.

There was some sort of shelf scene almost every year, but other ideas kept bubbling up: a full-size papier-mâché mummy was made in art class and entombed with great ceremony; a British fort built in the woods later became a station on the Underground Railway; bottles of coke and homemade candies were appropriately wrapped and decorated and sold as Tut's Tonic and Khufu's Karamels; full-size murals were painted; and much time was spent making maps, some of them pictorial.

And then there were the original skits, always humorous, which the children put together in two or three days, just for the fun of it, or to do in assembly. All groups loved to write nonsensical rhymes, which one child would usually read aloud while the others acted out the story in pantomime. The children found an amusing side to almost everything they studied and the skits were a fine outlet for their pre-adolescent humor. Occasionally the group liked a skit so much it was expanded and turned into a real play—for of all the activities connected with social studies, giving plays was the favorite.

After a number of weeks, reports would be finished and read aloud to the group. Although there was, of course, a wide range in the students' ability to make their reports clear and interesting, the group listened with great attentiveness to all but the longest and most boring efforts, of which there were few.

Discussions followed the reading of reports. Then tests were given which checked on factual information learned, but, more important, contained what the children labeled "thinking questions." These were often made up by the students themselves. I remember two: "Why did the Greeks love life so much and the Egyptians just think about death?" and "Why do you think the Colonists were able to lick the great British army?"

I discovered by accident how much children get out of a trip to a museum, historic site, or industrial plant if they already know a good deal about what they are going to see. The first year we studied Egypt, I tried to arrange a visit to the University of Pennsylvania Museum soon after school started and was dismayed to learn that the first appointment available was in November. When we finally arrived, the children knew so much about Egyptian gods and pharoahs, ahnks and hieroglyphics, mastabas and papyrus, and asked such good questions, that the docent was delighted and gave us an extra hour of her time.

Among the places we visited in or near Philadelphia were: Independence Hall, the Betsy Ross House, the Atwater Kent Museum (history of Philadelphia), William Penn's statue on top of City Hall (for a bird's-eye view of the city), the Art Museum, the Commercial Museum, Delaware County Historical Museum, a T.V. broadcasting station, a stocking factory, and plants making paper products, assembling automobiles, processing foods, and printing newspapers. One group made a survey of the ways people earned a living in Media, our nearest town. The children were especially pleased when a local dry-cleaning establishment cleaned their own dirty sweaters and jackets while they watched. We also attended civil trials (traffic cases) at the Delaware County Courthouse in Media, talked with lawyers and judges, and visited all the local government departments. On every trip the children were well prepared for what they would see.

Each year the children's undirected creative writing began to show that they had become really involved in what they were studying. For example:

63

SPHINX

The sphinx, just sitting, watching us.
What has he seen?
Just think, he has seen us and he has seen people
    thousands of years ago.
He's seen those two generations, and how many in between?
First watching the Egyptians, then watching us.
How mighty he must feel,
The grand and might sphinx—
    captured in a building!

                                         Cathy

THE ACROPOLIS

Rising above all other things, on top of a steep
    rocky cliff.
Watching over multitudes of crude houses,
Ruling many people,
Staring over miles of gray mountains,
Reaching to water, and land, and more water.
Then changing,
Aging, crumbling,
Seeing people and buildings change,
Looking thin against a sunset,
But still brave, mighty—
The acropolis, honoring her hero, ancient Greece.

                                       Cornelia

THE MACHINE AGE

I see wheels turning,
Cogs clanking,
Huge machines rumbling,
Cars and trucks growling,
Trains rushing,
Planes flashing,
Boats splashing,
Wires running, running,
    running,
From one place to another.

I hear clanking, roaring,
    rumbling, growling,
    splashing, clicking,
    thumping MACHINES!

                                       Jed

Thousands of machines coming at me,
Machines with big arms,
Machines with big brains,
Machines answering all problems.
The people aren't doing *anything*!

                                       Will

Writing poetry or doing skits, painting time-line pictures were all good ways of making the content of the social studies program a usable part of a child's total experience, but for the oldest group at The School in Rose Valley the only completely satisfying climax to any major part of our studies was the giving of a play.

All parts of the curriculum become involved when a play is in progress—art, crafts, music, creative writing, even math (for accurate measurements are needed if scenery is to fit and properties be usable). But the content of the older children's plays is almost always drawn from what they are studying in social studies, and many periods are devoted to the making and rehearsing of plays.

Why have we felt that dramatic experience is so important for our students? I believe that there are several values in this type of dramatics. Plays provide an opportunity for individual children to express their feelings, released, by virtue of being fictional characters, from the inhibiting pressure of speaking and behaving as they think adults want them to. At preschool level, dramatic play is spontaneous and continual. Being a mother, father or baby, a lion or a monkey, a fireman or a sailor, a small child acts out his feelings about himself and his world all day long. Singing and dancing games and the dramatizing of familiar stories let each child choose a role he likes and put into his characterization as much of himself as he wishes.

In the lower grades there is still much free dramatic play, and we encourage the acting out in pantomime of experiences and feelings. Short, simple plays give many a child the chance to discover that he can express himself as a cowboy or a goblin less self-consciously than in his own person. Our third grade's traditional, outdoor Indian play, which has a longer period of preparation and rehearsal, means becoming someone else for quite a while. A timid boy may turn for a time into a fierce warrior, or an over-aggressive little girl may become a gentle loving mother to her papoose.

At the older age levels, there are endless examples of a child expressing feelings that were normally hidden. A quiet, repressed sixth grade girl announced in a post-Revolutionary play that she hoped a bear had eaten her brother, and later gleefully chopped off her dolls' heads on an imaginary guillotine. A serious-minded boy turned into a fine comedian, capering about with a butterfly net as a teen-age Lord Fauntleroy in a gay-nineties sketch. A formerly stiff and self-conscious young actress let herself go, with loud mock sobs and gestures of wild despair, over her uninterested lover—"Matt o' the Pig Pen"; another child, who had felt at ease only in comic parts, did a moving scene as the former friend of an accused Salem witch. These are only a few examples of the surprising revelations about children that occur every time a play of their own making is given.

Rarely has a play been produced at The School in Rose Valley without a crisis of some sort. Robin Hood, always rehearsed in the school woods, is driven indoors by a June thunderstorm; the hero of another play comes down with the measles between afternoon and evening performances; the scenery collapses or the curtains won't pull; cues are not given or the record-player isn't started on time. One unforgettable improvised conversation, when this last mishap occurred during an Isis and Osiris play, began: "Where did you get such neat dancing girls?" "Oh, from a little joint down the river."

Probably the biggest crisis with which any group had to cope was when the music teacher was injured in an automobile accident on her way to play for quite an elaborate musical. The ten- and eleven-year-olds rose magnificently to the occasion and sang the whole thing a capella, with great success. Indeed the children have always surmounted difficulties and handled emergencies with imagination and poise, and the experience gained has carried over into other situations.

The creative opportunities inherent in the making of plays are many: Making up one's own part and helping with poetry and songs for the whole cast; building sets and constructing all sorts of properties; designing and painting scenery; making or adapting costumes. The children are not always dependent on words to express themselves creatively. The most moving play ever given at The School in Rose Valley was a pantomime, to music, about the Salem witch trials.

The youngest children show great ingenuity and imagination and feel no need for formal scenery, props or costumes. They use planks and boxes, playground apparatus and toys, and odds and ends from the costume chests with good results. This same ingenuity and imagination is displayed by older boys and girls who have painted some really beautiful scenery and have invented ways of making everything they needed from an Indian tepee to a *deus ex machina* platform, from convex Greek shields to a two-headed Chimera and a one-eyed Cyclops. One group made scene changing easy by using a plain gray backdrop to which they added, as required, different types of windows, a fireplace, a sampler, family portraits, etc., all painted on oaktag (light cardboard) and attached with Scotch tape and safety pins. There is something for everyone to "invent" when a play is in the making.

Children as young as five and six begin making up the dialogue needed in their plays, so that by the time they reach the oldest group it is a natural thing for them to do, and they are able to write plays, some of which show a depth of feeling and beauty of expression, or in the comedies, a sophisticated humor, unusual at elementary school level.

It is a temptation to quote at length, but the humor, especially,

66

does not come through well except as part of the whole play, so much of it depending on the acting and the interchanges between the players. Perhaps a verse from each of two musicals laid in the Middle Ages will give some hint of the sort of light-hearted satire our fifth and sixth graders find easy and fun to produce.

After falling in love, Matt 'o the Pig Pen sang:

> Oh, pigs can be a bore.
> They weren't that way before,
> But now that I love her
> I seem to discover
> What maidens and men are for.

The court jester, in the other play, decided to be an unhappy misfit, and made up a sad, sad song which began:

> Little gloomy jester, I.
> Riddles and joking I did try;
> Now I'm a failure and can't see why.
> Sad little jester, I.

One other example: At the end of a delightful take-off on all Greek myths (the nearsighted non-hero inadvertently slew the monster before the real hero arrived), a white-garbed Greek chorus chanted solemnly:

> To the palace of King Minos,
> Pericles he led the way.
> Famous now in song and story
> Are the happenings of that day,
> Bringing fame and winning glory
> For the hero of our play,
> Famous fame and glorious glory
> For the hero of our play.

In some of the serious plays, creative writing periods were used to compose much of the content. Sometimes an individual would work alone; sometimes a small group would pool ideas and dictate to the teacher. A dance about Space was based on such a group poem, which was read aloud during the dance by one of the girls, ending with:

> Man in space
> wondering which way to go
> staring into darkness
> turning to see only still more darkness
> the quiet is so quiet
> everything so strange . . . and wonderful
> then!

out of the darkness come unique beauties
whirling solar systems
flashing comets
huge stars moving slowly across the sky
desolate and quiet
yet filled with motion
then each one softens
and blends into darkness once more.

The boy who played Ihknaton in one of our Egyptian plays wrote the following prayer:

Oh, gracious and loving Aten, who watches over
   me and my people, hear me.
I have built this beautiful city where all men
   should dwell in happiness.
I have ended slavery in Egypt, for everyone is
   equal in your sight.
I have built temples in your honor, that all men
   might praise you and see your glory.
All these things have I done in your name, and yet
   the people do not respond.
No one is content.
There is hatred and strife in my country.
The priests, the generals crowd me from every side,
   asking me to make war and forsake you.
Why? Why has this happened when I have only carried
   out your wishes? Why do they not feel your love?
Have I done wrong? Have you forsaken us?
Oh, Aten, what can I do? Who can I turn to?

Probably the most completely satisfying project on which a large group of children can work together is a play. When a start is made, at six or seven, on longer and more organized productions, the children do not think of the play as a whole, but only of "me" and "my part." It takes executive ability and endless patience on the part of the teachers to help them function together. The children are, however, proud and pleased when the play is finally given. One first grade reported with honest joy in the school newspaper: "We gave our Christmas play. It was wonderful."

Even at ten and eleven years "my part" is still of great importance. In an ideal play for this age all roles should be leading ones. However, in the oldest groups there is a growing ability to see and understand the over-all picture and to realize that since they are writing the play themselves anyone can make himself a good role. Also, they know there will be other plays and there is an unwritten understanding that today's hero or heroine will take a minor role next time.

Involvement

From the day the plot of a forthcoming play is first outlined (either by the group as a whole or by a small, elected play-planning committee) until the final curtain falls there are endless opportunities for contributing to the success of the production. New and unexpected abilities appear for thinking of things to say and do. for directing rehearsals, for designing scenery, for inventing and making properties and costumes, for arranging the stage and getting the balky pull-curtains to work. The play gradually becomes "ours," all of it important, not just one's own part; and the children come to depend upon and appreciate the newly found talents of people not previously considered important.

While the oldest children tend to be very critical of their own performances, worrying over small mistakes not noticed by the audience, the group as a whole is elated after each successful play. There is a rewarding feeling of group unity and accomplishment which usually carries over into the classroom and playground.

Acting out experiences and, for older children, acquired information, is an essential part of the learning process. Judging from what they say, our graduates remember for years the plays in which they took part at The School in Rose Valley. Since, in the older groups, plays are based on what we have been studying, this means remembering quite a bit about such things as the American Indian civilizations, the Westward Migration, the Middle Ages, or the Greek gods. Once you have jousted in a medieval tournament, recited from a hornbook in a Puritan school, floated down a blue muslin river in a Chinese junk, or welcomed escaping slaves at a station on the Underground Railway, you have given reality to these far-away times and places by making them part of your personal experience.

Among the subjects of the plays and sketches produced at Rose Valley have been: cave men, American Indians, Egyptian history and mythology, the Roman Empire and the Middle Ages, Old Testament stories, and those of Christmas and Hannukah, the New World explorers, the Thirteen Colonies, the American Revolution, Westward Migration, the Civil War, the Gay Nineties, Space.

How exactly is a play "made"? There are no rules, no neat recipe for a teacher to follow. The process is never quite the same, nor is the result. However, a short step-by-step résumé of the evolution of two Egyptian plays may show the process as it might be (and *was* on at least one occasion).

In 1961 the oldest group consisted of twenty-four children, twelve sixth graders and twelve fifth graders. This group became tremendously interested in Egypt, so we stayed with that civilization for over two months. When many books had been read, many pictures and artifacts studied, reports written and read, time line pictures painted, trips taken to the University Museum, and a full-size papier-mâché mummy made and placed in a decorated burial chamber (formerly a goat house), it was obviously time for a play.

As usual, the first step was a group discussion as to what the play should be about. Immediately there was a sharp division of opinion. Most of the sixth graders wanted an action play, something exciting, like *Messenger to the Pharaoh* which had been read aloud to the class. Many of the fifth graders had been impressed by what they had learned about Ihknaton, and touched by his dream of one loving god and the tragic ending of that dream. After much argument, with neither side willing to give in, Charles, the leader of the Ihknaton faction, proposed that two plays be given. This was hailed as the perfect solution.

For the sake of convenience, since the two grades were separated at times each day, the fifth grade agreed to do *Ihknaton* and the sixth grade the other play, which was later christened *Khufu*. The whole production was called *Two Pharaohs*. Actually the whole group worked to some extent on both plays—painting scenery, making costumes and properties, and writing parts of the script. The usual committees were chosen to co-ordinate these activities, and two stage managers were elected.

The groups met separately to discuss the content of each play. The fifth grade decided to stick closely to Ihknaton's story, which was reviewed at this time. Four scenes were agreed upon:

  I. Ihknaton's visit to the *Street of the Craftsmen* when his beautiful city, Ahketaten, was new and prospering.
 II. *Ihknaton's Palace* when news came of the crumbling of the Egyptian empire and the conspiracy of the priests of Amon.
III. *Tutaknahaten's Quarters in the Palace*—Ihknaton's death is reported, and the priests take control of the prince.
 IV. *Street of Craftsmen*—the new pharaoh, now called Tutankhamon, departs with his retinue for Thebes; the craftsmen mourn the end of Ihknaton's dream.

A list of characters was drawn up. Everyone felt that Charles should be Ihknaton and that Loring should be his wife ("She looks most Egyptian"). When more than one child wanted a remaining part, informal try-outs were held and the loser accepted matter-of-factly the decision of his peers and chose another part to play. It was found that several additional craftsmen were needed and some of the sixth grade boys volunteered to be in both plays. Later the older ones asked a small, black-haired, fifth grade girl to be Khufu's daughter.

Meanwhile, the "Khufu" group was going through much the same process except that they had to make up their own plot. This turned out to be full of wicked enemies and nefarious schemes, eventually centering around the kidnapping of Khufu's daughter. The chief villian was Khufu's nephew, who wanted the throne for himself. Parts were chosen in the usual way, Willy becoming the Pharaoh and Jeff his treacherous nephew. (Will and Jeff had been the spokesmen for the Khufu group from the beginning of the discussion.) There were five scenes:

  I. Khufu's workroom in the palace.
 II. Palace garden—kidnapping scene.
III. Street scene before Temple of Set.
 IV. Khufu's workroom.
  V. Inside Temple of Set—the villains are caught!

Alone or in small groups, with or without a teacher, the children set to work making up their parts—most of which were not written down until later. After a day or two, when they had enough ideas to start with, they began putting the plays together, revising and adding new material as they went along, and figuring out what action was needed—where to stand, sit, walk, fight, or whatever the script required. Their only "professional" help was in this last area, from the assistant teacher who had had theatrical experience; the

71

children were not bound by her suggestions and sometimes over-ruled them. As soon as the children begin working together on a play, they call it rehearsing, as of course it is, but they are actually creating the play during these "rehearsals," and the words and action keep changing to some degree each time, often even in the final performance. For this reason the words of a play are seldom written down until after a number of rehearsals; in fact, a number of plays never had a written version.

The dialogue in *Khufu* delineated the characters and developed the plot. Since an understanding of Khufu's obsession with the building of his Great Pyramid was essential as background, the play opened and closed with a pantomime of workers pulling the great blocks of stone up the ramps. To create the mood for this pantomime, the "workers" were told to run fast twice around our large playing field. When they panted into the room, hot and sweaty, water was refused them. They collapsed on the floor in great indignation while the "nobles" walked contemptuously among them, sipping cold drinks. One child actually lapped up some spilled water from the floor. With little time to rest, they then pantomimed pulling the heavy blocks. Even when they were rested and no longer thirsty, the "workers" remembered how they had felt and were eager to express themselves in writing, as well as in pantomine. One of their poems was chanted at the end of the Khufu play:

> Sun sun sun sun
> Heat sun sweat
> The endless weight of burning blocks
> Pull pull
> So long so unbearably long
> The unmerciful sun beating down
> Aching exhaustion
> Weakness thirst
> Then the whip
> Biting—snarling cutting
> Pull pull
> Thrust the weight forward
> Pull pull
> So long so unbearably long

Much of the Ihknaton play was written during creative writing periods, in some cases by a child other than the one who later spoke the lines. This was a departure from our usual custom, but the children felt it appropriate for this particular play. All of the principal characters made up their own parts, really struggling to express what they were feeling. Charles was best able to do this and sometimes helped others. His prayer to Aten has already been quoted. Almost everyone tried writing something for the craftsmen to say, either in the first scene when they were proudly presenting

72

the gifts they had made for Ihknaton and Nefertiti, or at the end, as they bewailed the death of their dreams. There is not room to print any of these in full but a few lines may show how the children expressed the change of mood:

FIRST SCENE

WEAVER: Back and forth, back and forth goes my shuttle.
Oh, look at those brilliant colors!
Back and forth, back and forth, in and out—
Nothing is too good for the Pharoah Ihknaton, nothing.

COPPERSMITH: My work gleaming in the sunshine—the sun itself—
Like a shimmering ball of gold although it is just the finest copper.
The Queen Nefertiti orders me, a poor coppersmith,
(Imagine, me!) to make her a bowl.

LAST SCENE

WEAVER: No more back and forth goes my shuttle.
The Pharoah will not come for my lovely drape.
Ah no, for there is no Ihknaton.
There is no loving god.
Now I must go from this beautiful city,
Now I must go from this land of my dreams,
Go and scratch in the streets of Thebes.

COPPERSMITH: Ihknaton has not come to receive his gifts.
All I hear is the sharp voice of Amon, the god of the priests.
Ihknaton is dead and so is his fair city.
The sun has set.
There is nothing I can do, nowhere I can go.

When the scenery committee realized how many scenes there would be, its members wisely decided to make a single large backdrop which would give the feeling of being in ancient Egypt. Nut, the star-studded blue sky goddess, curved across the top of the finished scene and reached down the sides to meet the brown earth god, Seb, lying at the bottom. In between was the Nile, with its fishing boats and the white ibis and golden papyrus reeds for contrast. It was most effective.

White robes for the women and priests and white "kilts" for the men were cut from old sheets by the costume committee and the teachers, and were taken home to be sewed. After trying to work with real beads, the property committee settled for deep necklaces cut from oaktag and painted with rows of big colorful dots; armbands were made in the same way. Everyone wanted these bright adjuncts to the plain white costumes and an assembly line had to be set up, with Khufu himself doing most of the cutting and every-

73

one from Nefertiti to the High Priest of Set painting away madly. Old broom handles and pleated, decorated oaktag became Egyptian fans.

We spent over three weeks on these two plays, a longer time than usual. While the making of a play is going on, all social studies and English periods, as well as free periods and some recess times, are given to this activity. There were arguments, mistakes, and frustrations; the teacher lost her patience completely at one point, which, according to the children, is necessary if any play is to be a success. On the whole, however, these were busy, happy, satisfying weeks of preparation. The plays were finally given three times in one day, for an audience of the preschool and firstgrade children in the morning, for the older grades in the afternoon, and, in the evening, for parents, alumni, and friends. Far from being satiated, the actors had just one refrain: "We don't want it to be over." One said, "There's such an empty feeling when a play is finished. It's like losing a friend." The only way to cheer them up was to tell them that soon they would be doing a Greek play, which they'd enjoy just as much, or more.

From The School in Rose Valley's very first days, the staff has been sure, and has tried to make clear to successive generations of parents, that our plays are given for the benefit of the actors, not the audience. Always there are moments in rehearsals which are more moving or more hilarious than any which occur in the final performance. The children have their learning experiences and their fun during the preparations and rehearsals. They come, quite often, to think and feel themselves into the characters they are portraying so completely that this comes across to an audience; but this is a happy by-product not the main purpose of making and producing a play.

The children do deserve and enjoy an audience, and sometimes being such an audience is a learning experience for our parents. One father commented years ago: "most important, so it seemed to me, was the feeling I had that the participants were really in that Puritan schoolroom and in that Catholic church." More recently a mother wrote: "I found myself once more moved and carried away in a fashion never approximated by the many (adult written) children's plays I have sat through during my life. I wondered again what it is that evokes not merely recognition or admiration, but a mood or emotion in the observer. I don't mean that this happens all the time in Rose Valley plays. I merely mean that somehow this intangible, this magic is given a chance to happen. Our children's efforts are crude enough, but they are moving because they are a struggle toward a form of communication of themselves . . . and so a faint beginning glimmer of understanding of what the actual creation of a work of art is."

74

10

CREATIVE WRITING

PEG NOWELL

T<small>O READ AND EVALUATE</small> intelligently the enormous quantity of children's writing produced during the past forty years at The School in Rose Valley seemed so formidable a task that I decided to concentrate on the creative writing done during the fourteen years in which I taught the fifth and sixth grades. There are always a few children too inhibited, too lacking in self-confidence, or too little interested in the possibilities of words to write anything but the superficial, the banal, or the would-be humorous. However, in reading over the written output of those years, I was pleasantly surprised to discover how much the majority did reveal of themselves and how original and imaginative some of that revelation was.

All of the children loved to listen to what others had written, gave generous praise when it was deserved, and were almost too uncritical. Many of them, however, evaluated their own work judiciously, accepted the fact that they often failed to please themselves with what they wrote, and occasionally knew the joy of completely successful creation when something turned out to be, as one boy put it, "What I wanted to say and how I wanted it to sound."

Although I know best the work of ten- and eleven-year-olds, I have read much that younger Rose Valley children have written and mention it briefly.

Of course preschoolers do not write; but they did dictate to their teachers; and what they had to say was direct, uninhibited, and sometimes wildly imaginative.

A wall is a thing what you have at home what you bump into.
Gary (age three)

We have a lot of crocodiles and the crocodiles ate up all the grass. They climbed about that far up in our trees and broke all the branches. They broke all our boxes and the trains. And they ate up a boy. But they didn't eat me.

Rollie (age four)

By the time children are five and six years old they begin to be influenced by stories they have heard and read. We try to give them—and even the seven-year-olds—many opportunities to dictate, often using the older students for this purpose, so they can be as long-winded as they wish. At these ages, everything must be a story and, of course, must begin "Once upon a time." However, even when they retell favorite stories, they add original touches.

Once upon a time there was a mouse. One day he went up in an airplane. He saw three planets that he never saw before. These planets turned into Space Monsters. In his airplane he had a net, so he caught the Space Monsters in it and brought them down to earth and showed them to his mother. He remembered he had a jar of rocket tree seeds, so he planted them. In a few days they grew into a rocket tree. He noticed a button on the tree and he pushed it and a tank of gas came off. This tree was like a pine tree only the needles turned into rockets. He put the tank of gas in the rocket and flew into space again. . . .

John G. (age six)

Once upon a time there lived a big bad wolf who hadn't got married yet. He wanted to get married so he might have a baby. One day he went to the king of the forest. Maybe the king of the forest could help him. On his way he got lost. "Oh, dear me, what shall I do?" The next day he went back home, and what do you think he saw—a wife sitting in a rocking chair with a baby in her arms. So the big wolf and his wife lived happily ever after.

Carole (age seven)

Third and fourth graders have sufficiently mastered techniques to do most of their own writing. They still prefer the story form, but many of them discover the fun of rhyming words and get carried away with sound effects.

I love spring.
It's the thing
When I can zing
Out in spring.

Bill H. (age seven)

All eight- and nine-year-olds do not stay bogged down in jingles and derivative stories, and an imaginative teacher can often break this pattern for a whole group, sometimes by as simple a device as introducing Haiku, a Japanese poetry form using seventeen syllables. The following are two of many beautiful pieces of creative writing by a recent fourth grade set free and encouraged by a sensitive teacher:

76

It's so quiet.
It's so still.
But in the air floats a leaf.
Where is it going? Where?

I walk along the street,
I know I must meet death,
I must walk in the gutter
   and wear the star.
I know death awaits me,
And I must suffer hunger
   and beatings.
How can people be so cruel?

Audrey W.

By the time children reach fifth and sixth grades they have given up trying to compete with professional story writers and are ready to experiment with their own kind of written expression. How can a teacher best help them at this point? Mostly, I believe, by leaving undone those things which ought not to be done. Two recent books, *The Way It 'Spozed to Be* and *Hooked on Books,*[1] give dramatic proof that children can and will express themselves freely and creatively in written words if adult standards, for both form and content, are dispensed with, as they should be. I taught form—spelling, punctuation, and grammar—as a separate subject, and tried to establish a permissive atmosphere for creative expression in which the students could write whatever they wished, whenever they felt so inclined, without any regard for spelling, punctuation, neatness, or nonessentials. As a result, those who enjoyed putting their thoughts and feelings on paper produced some interesting work, but many wrote little or nothing.

There are many way in which the details of correct form can be made interesting (we once gave a lively assembly program on parts of speech), but acquiring skills is essentially a matter of drill and memorizing. The children did not hesitate to express their feelings about this part of the curriculum:

CAPITALS

CAPITALS ARE LARGE, USELESS, TERRIBLE THINGS.
The poor little words, their feelings are probably hurt.
WHY ARE SOME WORDS ALLOWED TO HAVE CAPITALS
   and not others?
it is just not fair!
i wouldn't give any words capitals if peg didn't make me.

Sally W.

I used to use "was" when I should have used "were."
Never knew how to change "you are" to "you're."

---

[1] J. Herndon, *The Way It 'Spozed to Be* (Simon & Shuster, 1967); D. Fader and E. McNeill, *Hooked on Books* (Putnam Co., 1968).

But now that Peg has shown us the ropes.
We no longer act like grammatical dopes.

Andrea H.

At intervals the students were asked to write paragraphs in correct form without regard to content. Most of them enlivened this disliked assignment with so much humor and imagination that the sentences were fun to read. There were many other opportunities to practice correct form. They included social studies reports, editorials and articles for the school newspaper, and letters asking for information or thanking a visiting speaker. Gradually, better form crept into the free creative writing without inhibiting its flow.

For several years I seemed to be doing a better job of teaching grammar than of encouraging creativity—which was not at all what I wanted. Then, with other staff members, I attended a class in creative writing led by Alexándra Docili, a dynamic and stimulating teacher. Not only did she find many ways of stirring up our senses and our emotions but she also required us to produce something each week. What we wrote might be good, bad, or (most often) indifferent, but we had to keep writing.

I soon began to apply what I was learning to my fifth and sixth grade students. They, too, were required to write something each week, no matter how short, no matter how uninspired. There were groans and complaints, but they wrote. Eventually, we evolved a system by which I suggested a subject every other week. There was no compulsion to use this subject and some never did. On the other hand, there were those who came to me every "free" week asking for "something to write about." The more the children wrote, the less of a chore it became for almost everyone. A great deal of the writing came to be done at home, probably because of greater privacy and fewer distractions. The last period on Fridays was set aside to hear each other's writings, but no one ever had to read his work aloud unless he wished to do so. We went even farther; any child could mark what he had written "Private" (for my eyes alone) and that bit of communication was shared with no one else. These honest and often poignant expressions of preadolescent feelings served an important purpose in giving each child a chance to tell what he was really thinking and feeling to an adult whom he trusted and with whom he was often willing to "talk it out" afterward.

To start the free writing experiment, I tried what we had done in the adult class. With closed eyes the children used, at different times, each of their other senses. They felt a variety of shapes and textures; smelled different odors; tasted things sweet, sour, salty, oily, bitter; listened in silence to the sounds of the classroom, playing field, nearby woods. After each experience they wrote words (not sentences) trying to describe what their senses had discovered. This was fun for everyone, but it also produced an astonished aware-

78

ness of our over-dependence on sight. One girl went on to write about how she would know it was spring if she were blind, and others followed suit, telling how they would know they were at the sea-shore, in an airplane, in the city, without using their eyes.

Another idea from our adult class which proved popular every year was to take any common, everyday object, get really to know it by using all five senses, and then write about it. A heightened awareness of things—both animate and inanimate—resulted, and also some imaginative ideas:

PAPER

Crisp, crunchy, crinkly.
Dry, gringy tasting.
Soft and wet in spitballs.
Light and annoying in paper planes.
Exciting news in newspapers.
Awful and mean in an arithmetic test.
Fun and wonderful in wrapping paper,
Colorful, bright, wrapped carefully
Around a tempting package for ME.

Louise F.

MY MITT

A yellow tan,
Big, with ferocious clapping jaws
like a lion's mouth.
A salty taste, but soft and smooth.
Protecting my hand from the ball.
Wonderful! My hand's best friend.

Jeff H.

MY ORANGE

Delicate ideas in an interwoven pattern,
Flashing orange,
A keen, sharp, penetrating smell.
Dents going with the grain.
Ever turning, bound with a perfect circumference.
Next white, its texture flowing out.
The opinionated skin holds its treasure—
tough, still, husky.
Out comes the flowing juice, a yellow river,
Luscious and smooth, never ceasing.

Emily I.

ONION GRASS

Terrible! ugly! Big stupid weed!
You pull out his hair,
But not his huge, white, flabby feet.
Sneering at you,
Showing you he's king of the weeds.
Aggravating!
Makes you so mad you want to extinguish it
from the earth.

79

Then you look at it again, looking up at you,
An innocent weed in an innocent lawn
   in an innocent world.

Melanie S.

A LEAF

Sharp, pricky things on its edges,
As many roads as a city,
Big superhighways,
And small, little country lanes.
Quite hilly, with its ups and downs.
When you turn the leaf over,
All the roads feel indented,
The big superhighways.
And the small, little country lanes.

Allen S.

Occasionally the children's response to "things" was startling and far beyond my own pedestrian flights of imagination, as when Tish, whose previous offerings had been fairly humdrum, pondered deeply about glass and came up with this:

PEOPLE

A pane of glass, fitted and puttied into a carefully made
   wooden frame.
The pane of glass reflects and shows all things inside it.
It was once a new, shiny and clean piece of glass, but now
   smudgy fingerprints tell of the dull, dirty life it has had.
It could some day break and shatter in hundreds of pieces.
The broken glass would be swept up, thrown away, forgotten.
It could have been a bottle or vase, but it was made for a
   window. And that makes all the difference.

Tish E.

Many others found meanings in the objects they studied:

WALLS

A wall has many sides to it for many reasons. It has paint
to make it turn to life, and wallpaper with bells and churches
to make it ring. Windows smile and bring laughter from the sun.
   The chairs rub and dig into the walls.
   The bed lies on hard ground, looking nowhere but to the
walls for comfort.
   The closet is dark and musty. Even though it has walls,
the light cannot reach it, so it does not dance with the trees,
the birds or the sun.
   Books tell of tales and true stories, but never do they
tell of the walls that laugh and gleam in the sun.
   We must load more and more into our room to bring happiness to the four lone walls.

Anne F.

A CLOCK

A massive structure, pushing people about.
It's what his face says that goes.
Standing erect, tall, straight;
Telling everybody to go to work, go to school.
Telling people just what!
A king, the ruler of people,
If people disobey his majesty, they pay.

Haig B.

Each year we talked a lot about our feelings—good and bad—
and wrote about them more and more freely:

ANGER AND SORROW

Anger—fury and madness!
Burning with hate,
I want to smash the world, or rule it.
I stamp and storm and scream at my friends.

Sadness is quiet and desolate,
Sorrow and loneliness.
I want to be forgiven and be friends again.
How can I face them? What shall I do?

Bill H.

FEAR

Fear is a tight feeling, because you want to do something
   but fear holds you back.
Fear will shut you into a shell if you let it overcome you.
Fear is a hard, struggling bug that tickles you when you
   meet up with something new.
But some people can pass fear without even looking at it.
If it weren't for these people we might still be in a cave,
   cooking wild rabbit in a dusty-looking pan.

Anne F.

FEAR

Fear is a feeling.
Fear is an awful feeling.
Fear is divided up into lots
   of little parts:
The fear of hate,
The fear of scare,
The fear of hope,
The fear of thinking,
The fear of happenings,
And most of all—
The fear of people.

Sandy H.

BOREDOM

Boredom brings twiddling of the fingers,
Pacing the room, long, sad faces,
Sighing, and leaning on elbows.

81

Then that brings dull moments,
Seconds as dry as dust on the ground.
The mind is covered with the fog of
    tiredness and weariness.
Nothing in the world matters.
There is just nothing to do, nothing to do.
The feeling of boredom is heavy.

Anne K.

THOUGHTS COMPILED IN A BAD MOOD TO FORM A DEPRESSING MUSE

The earth is flat for those who walk upon it and is the
center of the universe for those who occupy it.
Man is only sitting here, counting seconds flowing through
space until it is time for him to follow.
The world is made of opposites pushing one against the other.
Most people find an agreeable spot and glare across at the
dissenting opposite,
Until space is ready to have them follow the seconds into
the center of time.

Charles C.

ANGER

[Short excerpts from descriptive writings on this subject]

Anger is a balloon—
    when you blow it up too far
    and it pops.
Anger is a wind blowing
    inside a cloud,
Until it bursts,
Washing over everything,
Drowning everything.

Joy H.

A tornado,
getting stronger and stronger,
A monster,
creeping from person to
    person.

Haig B.

Hot! Tight!
Red and orange,
Burning, roaring,
A terrible bright fire,
Burning across my mind.

Cathy de M.

FEELINGS

Happiness is when you've finished a report.
Happiness is a good lunch. Happiness is being pitcher.
Happiness is when your hamster has babies.
Happiness is spring.
Happiness is when everyone is happy.

Sadness is after a fight.
Sadness is when no one likes you. Sadness is a rainy day.

82

Sadness is when you miss a ball.
Sadness is bare trees in winter.
Sadness is when everyone is sad.

Prue B.

Much harder than expressing one's own emotions was trying to "get inside" another person and understand his feelings. Not many even tried this, but two girls did put into words empathy not usually expected at such an early age:

A CHILD

A child, with his big wondering eyes,
His eager little body, ready to jump and play,
His short, round legs, wobbly, chubby—
The happy little cheerful one all through the day.

But then, when he gets sleepy,
He starts to yawn and grumble.
He starts to cry and fuss,
And cause a lot of trouble.

But when he wakes up next morning,
He's fresh and clean.
He's new and bright,
Ready to be himself again.

Laurie H.

A BOY IN SPRING

His thoughts rest on the green grass of the playing field
    that's bathing in the warm spring sun.
He longs for the rough feel of a hard ball and the handle
    of his thirty-four-inch slugger.
He scowls over menacing arithmetic pages, and smiles at spring.
Then recess comes!
He stretches every fiber and muscle in his body,
    in eagerness to play.
He runs out on the playing field in exhilerating happiness
    that spreads under the shining sun.

Cornelia B.

There were endless suggestions of subject matter which appealed to the children: colors, light, darkness (some actually wrote their reactions while sitting in pitch-dark rooms or closets), rain, snow, mud, animals, bugs, home, school, siblings, friends. Anything that had real meaning to a child was acceptable. But most interesting writing came when the children themselves felt the urge to communicate a special thought or feeling. Since our school and most of their homes were in partially rural areas, much of their thinking and feeling was about nature:

WIND

The wind, sweeping through the meadow,
Swiftly, silently,

Swishing over the grass,
Winding around buildings.
Turning, swerving, whipping, rambunctious—
Endlessly whirling.

The wind, roaring and blowing,
Plowing down dead trees,
Bending the living ones.
Even the mighty oak is kneeling to the wind.

The wind, elegant and soft,
Trying to puff down the apple blossoms,
Bumping gently against the grass,
Bending it only a tiny bit.
The wind is very weak.
The wind is almost dead.

Jon C.

SNOW

White flakes drop to the ground on a cold, shivering morning.
Really those flakes are little white castles,
Dainty points of crystal glass, all different shapes.
Temples prick from flakes, crystal clear and snowy white.

Sue W.

WINDSTORM

Wind, whistling through the trees,
Like a boy yelling, running through the woods.
A storm, breaking down houses and trees,
Like a big, angry boy knocking down his toy soldiers.
A windstorm roaring through trees,
Breaking down houses,
Like a big, angry boy yelling,
Knocking down his block towers.

Hugh L.

WINTER SEA

In and out with the spray
Of the cold winter waves,
In and out with the cold
    winter waves.
The tides turn
And the waves churn
Under the spray of the
    iciest days.

Jim E.

TREES

Sometimes trees are my
    only friends.
Trees are fun to climb;
    and sit next to.
They can soothe you,
And you can soothe them.

84

But then again, trees are
  my worst enemies,
Standing over me like
  enormous
  dictator mothers,
And I'm so small.

Sally W.

THE JUMP

Hay down below me.
I'm up aloft.
I feel like a butterfly
Ready to take off.
Then—one, two, three!
Off to the hay far below.
Woosh, I made it!
I did it—ME!
I jumped to down here
From way up aloft.

Tim J.

THE SEA

Deep, dark,
Queer, strange,
Wonderful.
Unknown, forbidden,
Beautiful.
New—frightening.
Old—soothing.
Musical, swaying,
Ever moving.

Nancy N.

Roaring, screeching, pounding,
In a magnificent rage.
Reaching higher, higher, higher.
Crashing down on jagged rocks,
Foaming and bubbling,
Snarling and spitting,
Like a furious tiger.
Then calming herself,
Withering and shrinking,
Crying softly,
Slowly rocking herself to sleep.

Louise F.

CORAL

Hard and pricky,
White, with a few stains from the sea.
It has a quiet, desolate look,
Or, when picked in movement, a wild look
  that was stopped dead
with the angry, swirling feeling
  cold upon hard stone.

Laura Beth W.

RAIN

On my roof rain sounds like little army men marching around.
The wind is rustling about, showing the leaves who is boss.
Inside my window one lonely little bug stands, to keep warm.
And I know what it is to be cold.

Anne F.

MOUNTAIN PEAK

The great spiral of rock,
Towering over me like an overseer
Looking down upon his slaves,
Or like on ocean looking down
  upon a baby fish
Trapped in his net of coral and seaweed.

Jim E.

A lot of writing had to do with school, particularly social studies and plays, and some of this is quoted in other chapters. There were always a few who enjoyed "light verse" just for the fun of it, while others relieved their feelings of annoyance or frustration by describing them humorously:

FISH

I caught a flat fish
In a swampy bay.
I put it in a dish
On a sunny day.
Phew!

Perry J.

WHEN DAYS WERE OLD

When days were old and knights
  were bold,
Electric stoves they did not
  have.
They froze to death,
Except the chef,
Who sat on top of the coals.

Andrea H.

WHY?

Why can't I hit a baseball
And sock it half a mile?
Why can't I hit a baseball
And let them chase it for a while?
Why can't I hit a baseball
As far as man can see?

But I guess I'm not Stan Musial—
I'm just plain me.

Andy D.

OLDEN DAYS

I wish I lived in the olden days.
I wish we did things in the olden ways.
I'd have a bed with a canopy,

86

Embroidered with flowers for all to see.
I'd have a stove that used wood for fuel.
I'd have a horse and maybe a mule.
I'd have my own rooster. I'd have my own cow.
I'd have my own goat and I'd have my own sow.
I'd have a cat and a dog or two,
And a flower garden of wonderful hue.
Oh, I wish I lived in the olden days.
I wish we did things in the olden ways.

Laurie A.

BEING A GIRL

✓ I wish I were a boy so I could play football.
The girls are allowed only two-handed touch,
Which really is not very much.
I wish I were a boy.

Boys are yelling, on hands and knees.
"He's got the ball! Don't fumble it, please!"
We sit on the sidelines, trying to shine.
I wish I were a boy.

What do the girls do? Just make the noise.
Who has the fun? Guess who? . . . the BOYS!

Emily I.

KERCHOO!

The wind blows against the trees.
The pollen makes me sneeze.
I blow my nose,
And think of those
Who have no allergies.

Perry J.

Before any of us had heard of Haiku some children used a similar form of their own accord. A few never needed more than half a dozen lines to express a thought or to make a picture in words. Others used this short form occasionally. Trying to write Haiku is excellent practice for children, as well as adults; even ten- and eleven-year-olds tend to be too verbose.

NIGHT

Night creeps up on you
  like a snake.
It is gloomy, dark,
  and endless.

Mark P.

SPRING

The flowers of May put on
  their summer sunsuits,
To have the warming sun
  beat down upon their breasts
  of yellow and brown.

Jim E.

87

MOUNTAINS

Towering masses of rock,
With gushing, icy streams.
Are the peaks
old, gossiping women?
Or are they
aged, forbidding men?

Prue B.

BOYS

Boys are dim, unpolished things,
But always ringing.

Carla L.

Several times each year we wrote as a group and used the results as choral reading. There were parts read by the girls, parts by the boys, and parts for individuals; but for all of the children it was a group experience they had recorded and wanted to share with others.

One September afternoon, the twenty-seven children in our group went into the woods behind the school; they were told to sit in a comfortable spot, close their eyes and *listen.* After about fifteen minutes, without any talking, they came back silently to the classroom and wrote down what they had heard. These auditory impressions were later combined and arranged by the teacher and used for a choral reading:

THE SCHOOL WOODS

All quiet at first . . . dark . . . quiet.
Then, faintly, softly, the sound of the wind
through the trees,
Sweeping through the trees like small waves
rippling the surface of the ocean.
Louder, louder,
Sounding like rain,
Then dying down,
Quiet again, darkness.
The creek, trickling gently,
The whistling and gurgling of the creek.
The caw of a crow, like a bad spot in a ripe banana
The shuffling of feet; the crunching of dry leaves.
Somewhere off in the distance a dog barks.
An airplane drones its endless drone.
The distant clap of boards,
The far-off cry of a bluejay.
Trickling water—rushing, splashing, bumping on stones.
The wind—weaving in and out through the leaves.
An acorn falling to the ground.
Steady quiet hum of crickets.
A small sneeze.
The tinny bang of a trashcan lid.
Breath coming from someone thinking.
People changing positions.

The nothing sound of a stone flying through the air—
    and then landing . . . crunch!
            The wind—
Blowing a loose leaf and making it roll over and over
    like a wheel rolling through broken glass.
A car on the road, sounding just like a car on a lonely
    road should.
A clear call from a bird nearby.
Very softly the leaves fall to the ground, with a light
    ploy to the ground.
            The wind—
Like a heavy rainfall beating down through the leaves,
Like clashing ocean waves, like a crackling fire.
        Content—happy—satisfied—comforted—
(Sudden sharp shock of a voice ending the silence.)
I wish I were out there again, in that world of peace.

One group composition started from casual lunchtime conversation on the first really warm spring day in 1961. It grew through several days of discussion and contribution and was given in the next school assembly as a choral reading. I hope this somewhat condensed version keeps the feeling of a Rose Valley spring which— mud and all—so permeated the original.

SPRING AT THE SCHOOL IN ROSE VALLEY

No more bulky coats,
No more heavy boots,
No more soggy pants.
        Free! Free! Free!
Rose Valley T shirts,
Sweaters tied round your waist,
Shorts! Bare legs!
Running! Throwing! Kicking!
        Fuzzy pussywillows,
        The first crocus,
        Violets, daffodils,
        Fragrant apple blossoms,
        Calm, cool grass.
First and worst is the mud!
        A ladybug crawling up your arm,
        The buzz of a bee,
        The sting of a wasp,
        The happy peeping of peepers.
The squish of mud under your shoes.
The squush as you sink in the mud.
        The good, honest smell of the earth,
        Warm air and cool breezes,
        Tiny green buds covering the trees,
        Bursting out of their wintry shells.
First there's mud outside.
Then there's mud inside.
        The clang of hammers on nails
        As the Four's build a treehouse.
        The joyous barking of dogs,
        The shouts from the playing field.

89

Then the mud inside dries and is swept out,
Only to come in again, when it rains, on our boots.

The spring song of a robin,
The sharp, piercing cry of a pheasant,
The creaking of a starling.
New baby birds sticking their heads out
    for food.
The delicious smell of bacon sizzling
    over a camp fire.
The luscious, slightly-burned bacon you
    have so carefully cooked.
The fizzle of a birdwalk pancake—
    a scrambled pancake!

The lazy feeling in spring,
A soft wind brushing gently across my face,
The drone of a bee in the appleblossoms.
I can't work.
I've got spring fever.

The whizz of a baseball,
The crack of a bat,
The muffled plop of the ball in a glove.
I can feel when I'm going to be out.
        Softball!
A peg to first base,
A grounder going through your legs,
The always present "strike three."
When I'm out I can feel everyone staring at me.
        Softball!
The sweet sound of wood meeting horsehide.
The fatal sound of glass shattering!
Girls screaming!
Three months' allowance shot to pieces.
        Softball!

Happy voices of kids at the May Fair,
Tinny sound of the merry-go-round,
Siren sound of the big red fire engine.
Juicy hotdogs broiling,
Barbecued sandwiches,
Sucked lemons flying through the air.
The colors floating round and round,
Blending into a fascinating May Pole.
Blare of the loudspeaker—
"Oldest Group sword dance next!"
Bright, whirling skirts,
Fast movement of feet,
Burnished swords glittering and twirling
    in the air.
        The clash of swords!
        Risen stars!
        Clapping hands.

        Then the music stops.
        The sword dance is over.
        The sad, sad thought,
"This is our last Rose Valley spring."

We read poetry, too, silently and aloud—everything from Shake-speare to A. A. Milne, from Robert Frost to Edward Lear. The children sometimes memorized their favorite poems. We talked a lot about "words," their sounds, their shades of meaning, their origins, and even invented some words of our own. Sometimes the teacher and her assistant tried writing "poems," and their efforts were received in the same spirit as those of any member of the group. Constructive criticism was given if a child seemed ready for it, but always with the idea that something good might be made even better. Whether any of these things helped to keep the children writing I do not know. I do believe, however, that what mattered most was that each child knew that whatever he wrote would be not just accepted but valued by all who read or heard it.

11

ART AS A FUNDAMENTAL

ART, IN THE MOST comprehensive meaning of the word, permeated all of our school program, though The School in Rose Valley is in no sense an art school, nor especially dependent upon artists. We were concerned with keeping the child lively, alert, curious, and creative, and to that end made art a part of everything.

This aspect of progressive education has always been difficult for traditionalists to understand. Having considered the arts as fun things, as extras to be added only when and if the necessary subject matter had been covered, they found it natural to suspect that progressives were abdicating, were tired of doing the hard work, and determined to do only what was fun. But when time had passed and there had been enough comparative testing done to find that in academic subjects the progressive school children did as well as, and often much better than, their peers in traditional schools, there was increased interest in the new approach.[1]

The idea of art as a foundation of education needs definition of both education and art. There are two views of education; one, that a man should be educated to be what he is, and the other, to be what he is not. The first retains man's idiosyncrasies, the second tries to eradicate all those that do not conform to the mores of the society of which he is a part. The progressives took the first view, and therefore adopted the broad definition of art as concerned not only with form, color, and movement in a variety of media, but with the uniqueness of the individual. As educators we were interested in all

[1] See J. Paul Leonard and Alvin C. Eurich, *An Evaluation of Modern Education* (Appleton-Century, 1942). Wilfred Aiken, *The Story of the Eight-Year Study* (Harper Bros., 1942), chap. 5.

means of expression, in everything that contributed to the development of intelligence and judgment—to the growth of a whole person.

What does this mean to a teacher? It means that he must know in his own person what the creative process feels like, if he is going to understand it in children. He should have had experience with an activity so engrossing he forgets time and place in his struggle with the material. This can happen through painting, writing, sculpture, music, dancing, gardening, designing, cooking. The experience is deeply felt and somehow changes him. He has discovered something about the material.

This is so important that I feel safe in saying that anyone can be trusted with children who has this understanding about his own experience and who is experiencing this creative process constantly in his own person. And there is a great deal of risk in trusting a teacher who is not being thus educated. This doesn't mean, however, that we at Rose Valley were creative artists, but we did realize that children are natural artists. We could let the creative process happen to them, if we knew enough about it. And since this process might involve any of a variety of media, we made work with wood, paint, clay, and words a part of the daily program.

Our wood-working shop was a place where time was always forgotten. It was full of children all day and every day. Just to go in there made the child's eyes sparkle as he felt the excitement of that wall of tools and the itch to use them. The challenge of hammer and nails was irresistible, and when, after a try at hitting a nail, he found he could make two pieces of wood stay together, he was in production. The three-year-old might bore holes for some time just to feel the tool; then nail two sticks together and call it a horse or an airplane, clutching it eagerly—"This is mine. I made it." Only someone who has had a similar experience knows the feeling.

Because the child wanted that feeling he learned the language of tools—what each one meant, how each one could be controlled. It is a heady experience, learning to control. Up to this point, usually the only method he had used successfully was pulling emotional strings—crying, kicking, begging—but this new method of control wasn't based on emotion. He had to learn how the tool worked; then he could make it do his bidding. His output of boats, airplanes, cars, engines, and dump trucks was endless, and they certainly could not be described as art objects; but we urged parents not to be too critical, as the process and eagerness to go on, not the product, were important. As long as the child was eager to produce, he was getting an appreciation of wood, of tools, and of his own power. The use of his imagination in our shop would stimulate its use in other areas.

Shop work was also an important element in social experience. Children were usually helping one another, or helping the adults, to build something—a hen house, a place to store tricycles, a rabbit hutch, pig pen, brick playhouse, goat house, outdoor pool, garden tool house, or shack with bunks for over-night camp-outs. They helped build a classroom (*The Mushroom*, of which *The Chip* is the remainder), helped build the 1942 addition to *The Chip* (four rooms on the east end), and in a summer camp built the *Field House*.

One shop report of ten- and eleven-year-olds shows that work was done for both individual and social ends. Projects included: baseball bases and backstop, jumping standards, small rowing punts, boxes, stools, chairs, a work desk, tables, doll's houses, toy trains, an astrolabe, frames for scenery, swords and spears for properties, model airplanes, gadgets with no apparent purposes, and other things crude in form and lacking in adult meaning but interesting enough for a time to the child who made them.

Mr. Rawson, who had been influential in introducing shops in Friends Schools, emphasized the importance of simple and inexpensive equipment, partly to answer the objection of schools that a shop was too expensive to be justified in an elementary school, and partly because of the intrinsic value of home-made things. Making something that was needed supplied a reason for learning how to make it; and the work of parents and teachers in constructing the buildings, devising outdoor and indoor apparatus, working in the shop on their own projects, made the children eager to be doing the same kinds of things. Mr. Rawson gave each child a good feeling about himself and his ability, and they loved him. When he died during the school term, the children came to me and said, "You shouldn't have let Mister die. We needed him." As we sat together and talked, the children told anecdotes of what they had done with him and how they had enjoyed his funny stories. Although grieving, they remembered him happily.

Mr. Freeman came into the school from Pendle Hill. One of the administrators said to me, "This man is too good for us; he ought to be working with children. Can't you use him at Rose Valley?" We could. For fourteen years he managed the shop and made possible the continuation of the buildings (such as play houses, goat house, and pig pen) so necessary to a school like this. He made jungle gyms and horizontal ladders, devised playground equipment out of old parts—a merry-go-round from an old automobile wheel axle, an airplane from boxes and a steering wheel. He made a fleet of small wheelbarrows for the preschool and had children making their own wheeled toys. If a teacher or a child wanted a piece of apparatus or odd contraption he would find a way to make it. His good humor made the shop a pleasant place.

Bernie Fierro, who was an art teacher, came to the shop when Mr. Freeman retired. He continued to encourage building. One September, on the playground outside the shop there loomed a tall pole

94

left by the previous May fair committee—planted solidly for a greased pole stunt. He consulted with the children as to what to do with it. The result was *The Apple Core*, a sixteen-foot ship built by the second and third grades, complete with crow's nest and a cabin below deck. This took a long time to make, as did the covered bridge, a project of the older children, built over the gully between the main building and the woods. There have been other projects— the Trojan horse, the Ziggurat temple, the Indian log house, and a modern eight-by-sixteen-foot structure of their own design outside the sixth grade's classroom.

Music, too, was basic to the program. The body has its natural rhythms responding to the rhythms of life around it, and these must be respected. The expression "being in tune" describes a spiritual relationship, a sensitivity that aids perception. A normal child skips and sings, and in many good homes music is a basic ingredient of family life. The good school needs music too. There is a contagious enthusiasm that bubbles up in singing, that makes a daily dose desirable and carries over into other activities. So we sang every morning.

Cecil Sharp, an English musician, was important to us in the beginning because he was then completing a life work of collecting old English songs and dances from northern England and our Appalachian mountains. These combined good music with genuine folk tales and they formed the core of our singing. We added other good songs, found in odd places, and finally we mimeographed the collection and put them together in a book. Children were introduced to musical structure, starting with rounds, going to part-singing and descants, and finally to group work. The *Ballad for Americans* became a sixth grade favorite, sung by the children as if they had written the music and the words; it was part of them.

Dancing began with moving to music and gradually the child added pantomime. Little by little he learned the technique of musical body movement as well as the forms of musical language, so that he could use them on his own. He worked on answers to such questions as, how can my body illustrate a whole note? A quarter note? Can I do both at the same time? The children used dancing to express ideas and moods, as much as they used paint or clay. If a water wheel was difficult to show by picture, why not dance it? One whole three-act play about Salem witchcraft was done with only pantomime and music, the most moving in the school's history.

Along with this kind of dancing came the English country dances, and here again we were indebted to Cecil Sharp for his excellent harmonizing of the old tunes and the varied assortment of dances from Brighton Camp to Step Stately, Newcastle and Christ Church Bells that were enjoyed by the parents in the evening class as much as by the children at school. Often school parties consisted of parents and children doing English country dancing. The most difficult, the Morris and Sword, done only by the older children because of the vigorous and exacting movements, has survived in the May Day sword dances.

Fortunately the school was rich in talented parents, talented not only in the arts but in dealing with children. Classroom teachers early determined to have a class for themselves in which they could experiment: the first was in making clay pots, dishes, etc., and the most recent was a class in poetry writing with Alex Docili. Teachers have agreed with Sylvia Ashton-Warner that keeping open the creative vent was important and have felt that their own attempts at creative work helped immeasurably in teaching.

Art classes were scheduled, as were shop periods, at definite times under a special teacher, but the activities with art materials spilled over into the classroom every day, for children normally express themselves in color and form and need these outlets. If a report of a trip was in progress what better way to make your audience see what you saw than to paint a picture or make a model? If a period, or a historical event was to be dramatized, action often began as a mural that might emerge finally as scenery. A time-line frieze around the top of the wall could fix in mind historical sequence, and was also memorable for vivid color schemes. However, good painting and modeling does not just happen; someone must teach. The following article, written for our *Parents Bulletin* in March 1967 by Shirley Tassencourt, who taught with us from 1962–67, gives an idea of how one good teacher worked:

THE CARE AND NUTURE OF THE YOUNG ARTIST

I don't know what an art program should or shouldn't be, just as I don't know how one should draw a tree. Each teacher has to find his own way of communicating things he knows, things he suspects. Hopefully, in art, the teacher has had enough personal experience with form with expression to support experimentation wisely and to encourage students to work beyond cultural expectation.

When expression is truly individual there is no cultural precedent, no "imitated" to measure by. If in the home there is little knowledge of the abstract visual aesthetic, there is only the art teacher to hold the child in valuing and trusting the aesthetic happening. I think one of the most important functions of the art teacher is to verbalize, point to, and exhibit aesthetic dynamics in simple ways. I've seen such strength come to the children's art work when they trust their "full out" expression. In teaching art, as in many activities, the harder you do it the worse it gets. However, the harder you mean it, really care, the better it gets. As long as the children are moving well by themselves, I stay at the border of activity. If they begin to stray into paths of non-involvement or picayune art practices, then I start nipping heels.

There really is nothing one can teach about color and design, for if the picture is really good it is because it has grown out of an intimate expression—out of a sensitive experiencing. In both the areas

96

of color and design, these children run rings around most art teachers, so what is left to teach? My most important function here is to recognize and share with the other students, by means of exhibit or a few words, a support of these good happenings. These are often not recognized or especially enjoyed in the larger community, probably because they (the children's art) lack technique, finish.

The business of accurate draftsmanship, cleverness, neatness may get in the way of strong, vibrant expression. Some would argue that such a calamity may well be the pitfall of some over-controlled artist, but surely not these little children. Around fourth grade an insidious thing creeps into children's art work. The hand that flew across the paper tightens, the knuckles blanch, the pencil deeply scores the little corner of the paper where it is being worked. Where formerly, with color and proportions a bit askew, the child was able to reproduce life, now with great determination he creates *une nature morte*.

This is where I earn my salary, yea, verily, more than my salary. I don't rush in with "No, No. Never, No, No!" One of the child's impulses is sound, i.e., the desire for better communication—(when you say *dog* you want it to sound like *dog* to others). Instead, at this point I modify the program. I mumble things like, "Today we're going to pose for each other, very quick poses." The answer is, "But I can't draw people." "Perhaps you mean you can't draw them so they look good. Did I ever say you had to draw something so it looks good? Just to make sure you don't worry too much about what's going to happen on that sheet of paper, don't even look at the paper while you draw. Keep your eye on the contour of the figure. Let your brush move just as your eye moves—see—around the arm, across the shoulder, up the neck. If the line goes off the page, OK. If not, OK. Only two things are important: that you relax and let your body move with the drawing, and that you concentrate very hard with your eyes."

There are many other ways of working on this problem. Sometimes I bully the child; sometimes I paint with him; with certain children I just stand back and wait. It always takes time, often a year or two for a child to regain the vibrance and feeling of spontaneity that tends to be lost at about the fourth grade. I feel good as an art teacher if most of my sixth grade class is "swinging" (translated as working with direct spontaneity and with good form and content).

Anything can be an art material. An important understanding is that one's whole environment has aesthetic potential. To reinforce this concept we use many different materials in a wide variety of ways: the senses ("draw what you feel in this bag"); the imagination ("make a picture of a dream"); the psyche ("here are three objects—put them in a picture"); past experiences ("draw some feeling you had—cold, quiet, lost, dizzy"); present experiences ("make a zoo drawing, and action sketches, a still life, a drawing of some music, poetry").

Clay, perhaps the most important medium, is easily the children's most popular choice in free periods. Children have a natural affinity for clay. Many ways of using clay should be demonstrated and encouraged. The year I took a course in pottery the quality and quantity of ceramics work at the School in Rose Valley improved.

Studio days, or "the free use of any materials" are a regular occurrence in some classes; in others, an occasional one. The strongest, most exciting work usually occurs when the class is stimulated or motivated by a group focus or project. The challenge of self-direction or peer-direction is not always welcomed by pupils, as reflected by this conversation with my daughter: "What do we do in art, tomorrow, Mom?"

"Anything you want."

"What else? That's too hard."

These are some of the ways we tried to keep the children's creative inclinations active. In making art a fundamental part of our school program, our attitude was that of Schiller, who wrote in his *Letters on the Aesthetic Education of Man,* "Man only plays when he is a man in the fullest meaning of the word, and is only completely man when he is playing."

An illustration of "the creative process happening" was reported by a parent in the school bulletin in 1960.

WE HEARD AMERICA SINGING

On February 5th the 9's, 10's, and 11's presented a dance program directed by Ronne Arnold, (a teacher from West Philadelphia, now the director of the Australian Contemporary Dance Company in Sydney, Austrialia). The work performed was an original interpretation of selections from the Kleinsinger Cantata to words of Walt Whitman *I Hear America Singing.* The class had expected to give a finished production at the end of the year. At this half-way point, without costumes, they were presenting a stage in the development of the whole idea, and so the assembly was conducted essentially as one of the weekly sessions with Ronne.

The intensity of effort of all the children was remarkable; their talents varied, but every performer plainly put forth his best. Walt Whitman walked majestic through the land.

"I tramp a perpetual journey (come listen all)
My signs are a rain-proof coat, good shoes, and a
staff cut from the woods, . . ."

At the opening of three scenes were the words, "I hear America Singing, the varied carols I hear." Individual performers came to life to be, "mechanics . . . the carpenter . . . the mason . . . boatman . . . deckhand . . . shoemaker . . . hatter . . . woodcutter . . . ploughboy . . . the mother . . . the young wife at work . . . the girl sewing or washing . . . Each singing what belongs to him or her and to none else . . ."

I could see strong men, grown women proudly working, and even when I fixed my attention on individuals the spell was not broken. I saw no self-conscious side glances or smiles; each pupil was totally absorbed in his or her interpretation of the assumed role.

The first scene was the most finished, but in the course of the assembly we saw all stages in the development of the production. In some places Ronne gave cues and helped mark transitions; in others, he stepped in alongside an individual to lead him through a particular bit, and toward the end he substituted in Walt Whitman's part. Always he remained inconspicuous and yet was there when needed.

To find what qualities in Ronne that made his handling of the group such a fine example of creative education, I reread part of

98

Gilbert Highet's *The Art of Teaching.* "The first essential of good teaching . . . is (that) the teacher must know his subject, . . . the second is that he must like it . . . the third . . . is to like the pupils." Two other qualities of a good teacher that Highet points out are humor and kindness. All these demands Ronne meets. Dancing is the essence of his life and communication through this medium his greatest joy.

To illustrate and interpret in modern dance requires that these words of Whitman's be understood. The process of looking hard through the poet's eyes at the varied face and heart of America must have resulted in a new appreciation of the concept of Democracy.

We in the audience were given new sights into Whitman's poetry and the children must have achieved an appreciation of his poetry and of his vision of America.

12

REPORTS INSTEAD OF GRADES

GRADING SYSTEMS IN SCHOOLS often have changed along with the thinking about education. One common system has been to grade on a percentage basis, from zero to 100, with 75 as the lowest "passing" mark. This system was appropriate so long as education was thought of as a matter of memorizing subject matter and of acquiring skills that could be measured quantitatively. It worked after a fashion, but it gave the impression that the whole process was deceptively simple, that it was merely a matter of passing examinations—and it *was* mostly just that.

As educators gear their thinking to growth processes in children, however, they become aware that something more than percentages or symbols such as "A" or "C" or "F" is necessary if a child and his parents are to have meaningful reports of the child's educational progress. At the same time, there has been a trend away from competition as a motive and a growing emphasis on reports that will give an idea of how a child is developing, and what are his strengths and his weaknesses. These reports should also help the pupil get on to the next step, whether it is in arithmetic computation or in accepting people of different racial or religious backgrounds. A good report will give at least some indication of the basic concepts of education, and of children, in the school.

We always tried to keep in mind certain concepts about child development. For example, one of these was that human development proceeds through definite stages, and each child goes through these stages at his own pace, and this must be taken into consideration in educating him. This pace is to a considerable extent inherent in the individual child, although, of course, it is easy to slow it down with unfavorable influences, or to speed it up by providing a favorable environment. We tried to provide this favorable environment—one that would stimulate curiosity and learning.

100

We realized that a slow beginning does not necessarily mean a poor student (see the story of Slocum, chapter 16), any more than rapid acceleration necessarily means a good student. These differences are easily observed in any school and illustrate one aspect of the individual differences among children that must always be taken into consideration.

We were conscious, too, that in his development a child typically can be expected to reach plateaus and to back-track. He may rest, or even go back to a younger pattern, before he finally relinquishes it. It is important that the child feel there is no hurry. After all, he has some twenty years in which to gain physical maturity and the emotional maturity that should go with it. Let him savor each stage as he goes along. This may insure that he will not hark back to some infant stage in later life, but go on growing toward maturity.

Growth takes place in every phase of his activity and of his thinking. He changes his patterns in eating and sleeping, as well as his attitudes about responsibility, about himself, his family, the opposite sex, about Santa Claus, death, and religion. Schools should be aware of these kinds of growth as well as the growth in understanding and in ability to use academic knowledge, because arrested growth in any area of the personality affects growth of the whole.

One of the best evidences of growth is the child's absorption in his work. A report should give the parent an idea of where the child best achieves this and at what points he is blocked from achieving it. Normal growth is possible, without marks or grades as incentives. If bribes or punishments have to be resorted to, something is wrong.

Growth in academic skills is closely related to growth in emotional maturity. The only thing that should satisfy a parent or a teacher is a report—not merely a "grade"—on all phases of a child's progress, since achievement in school is the function of the total growth of the child.

Writing periodic reports on children is a difficult and delicate task, for the teacher is giving the parents his estimate of their child, and he may touch sensitive spots. Since the parents do not write reports (but if they did, they might touch sensitive spots for teachers), it is a good idea for parents and teachers to get together and understand how each is working. For this reason, we made a rule that all reports would be discussed with both parents, not just with the mother. Although this meant giving much outside time to home conferences, teachers willingly gave it when they discovered how important it was for them and for the children to get the parents' point of view and to see the child's place in the family. In our preschool group, teachers visited every incoming child at home before school began.

In our reports, we focused on how the child functioned physically, emotionally, and socially, for these points determined the ease with which he learned. We also reported, of course, on academic work and special subjects. When standard achievement tests were given (twice a year from the third through sixth grades) test results were included in reports with gains or losses from previous tests being shown.

Here are some sample reports:

LYDIA (a four-year-old whose mother worked in the school).

Physical State: Lydia is a beautifully coordinated little girl who bounces into the room with a greeting each morning and stays in motion the rest of the day. She moves like a dancer—light on her toes—and it almost seems as if there are springs in her feet! She is skillful on all of the outdoor equipment and loves the see-saw, the boards and boxes, the swing and the jungle gym. Running, climbing, jumping are all part of the play with friends, that continues through the day. Her health has been good and she has plenty of energy.

Lydia eats a moderate lunch. Sometimes she settles right down to sleep at rest time, but more often she wiggles and giggles for a while before sleep comes. She will often nap for ten or fifteen minutes at the end of rest and wake refreshed.

Social Relationships: Lydia loves to be with children, usually selects one friend at a time. She is one of the regulars in the doll corner and the dress-up clothes become part of her daily school outfit. She is easily stimulated by other children and most sensitive to any rebuffs, real or imagined. When Leo and Rosalind issue a special invitation for her to join them, she is glad to do so, but a mean remark from them can really set her off. Actually she is busy with friends she enjoys, most of the time, and Leo's and Rosalind's friendship isn't that important to her. On days when she is moody and out of sorts she has a hard time playing with anybody, does a lot of kicking and hitting or leading others in a verbal attack on Cassie. Lydia is friendly with her teachers but not overly dependent on us.

Emotional State: All of Lydia's feelings are changeable and on the surface. She can be loving and affectionate one minute, and furious the next. Two or three times a day she will say, "I want to go to see my Mommie," sometimes just to give her a kiss, sometimes because she is hurt or unhappy, or sometimes to avoid an unpleasant job in the room. We try to hold these visits to a minimum but Lydia obviously wants and needs to be in contact with her mother.

Work Habits and Routines: Lydia loves all the art materials and is eager to join whatever project is going on at the moment using paints, collage, crayons, clay, or dough. When she really gets involved, she will work for long periods of time and her pictures are exceptionally lovely. When her mood is off, she will put layer after layer of paint on the paper, blend it all together with her fingers, then fold the paper two or three times—very different from the careful work of another day. She loves the dance and dramatics; her movement is free and spontaneous. She goes to shop occasionally but isn't always able to finish what she begins.

When there's work to be done, Lydia tries to skip out of the room, but when held to a job she can finish it quickly. She can usually manage her outdoor clothing independently. She moves easily through the routines of the day with few teacher reminders.

102

She is a solid and important member of the' group and participates fully in all parts of the program.

This mercurial four-year-old might have created a problem, with her mother working in the school, but because the teachers and mother acted wisely, there was no problem.

A seven-year-old's first semester report in second grade, with a follow-up in the sixth grade:

Physical State: Lorraine seems in good physical condition, having had few colds.and absences from school. She has plenty of energy and eats and rests well.

Social Relationships: It is only in the area of individual-to-individual relationships that Lorraine seems to have any difficulties. Her attitude toward others at the beginning of the year was not very appreciative, friendly, or considerate except for one bosom companion, Jennifer. Mention of this at the home conference brought much cooperation in trying to broaden Lorraine's social relationships and she now seems more willing to include all the girls among her friends. There seems to be a real conflict between the desire for warmth in relationships with others and the seeming security of extreme independence. ("I don't need anybody for anything, and I don't expect anybody to need anything from me.") Except for a tendency to look for "giggling" situations in the group, Lorraine functions well in the group as a whole. She accepts and carries out responsibilities, is not an outstanding leader, but neither an uncritical follower, and cooperates in large and small group activities (except sometimes refusing to dance).

Emotional Stability: Except in the area of personal social relationships, Lorraine seems generally confident, always willing to try a job even though it may appear difficult. She can accept criticism, but is fairly competitive—perhaps too proud that she was an early reader and "is good in arithmetic." She may even rush so to beat in arithmetic that she turns in a highly inaccurate piece of work.

Work Habits: Lorraine's work habits are excellent. She shows interest in group projects, curiosity to gather information, and seems very observant. She is thorough, accurate, conscientious, and very self-reliant about day-to-day assignments. She has an active imagination and produces stories very easily, although she has not yet loosened up and "let go" in art.

Academic Work: Social Studies: Participates, shows interest, and contributes well.

Arithmetic: She understands well the concepts taught and is accurate with the number combinations when she is in not too much of a hurry. She can apply the knowledge logically to simple problem solving.

Language: Very competent; voracious reader. Spelling advanced and accurate within the limits of the few spelling tools given so far. In creative writing she produces imaginative pieces very easily. Penmanship is good.

Special Subjects: Art: Lorraine has fine creative ability and a natural response to all art media. Usually too much concerned with people around her. Works best alone.

Music: Sings more than in previous years and seems to enjoy music more. Also shows more enthusiasm for dancing. Is more cooperative.

103

Shop: Hasn't been going.
Science: Interested and able. Doesn't volunteer for demonstrations, but can be counted on to do her part.

Lorraine continued to do excellent work but her fourth grade teacher reported: "Intermittently her behavior suggests that she has doubts about her acceptance by the others. We hope that in time she becomes fully aware of her marked abilities and through them can find easier relationship with her peers."

In the fifth grade, the teachers wrote: "improving but still to be worked for: tolerance, understanding, and kindness of human relations."

The sixth grade report follows:

Lorraine's two years in the Oldest Group (fifth and sixth grades) have been most successful and, I believe, happy ones. Her fine academic record is well deserved but we are even more delighted with her growing ability to express herself freely and spontaneously in creative writing, in all forms of art work, in acting and even in social relationships, the least easy field for her.

Social studies was the subject in which Lorraine showed the greatest improvement this year; her reports on the Greek theater and the Renaissance were remarkably good for a sixth-grader, and she made an average of 97% on the five social studies tests, which were *not* at all easy. She also continued to do outstanding work in mathematics and creative writing and has shown steady improvement in language skills, even spelling, when she is careful.

French: Consistent and dependable; excellent progress.
Science: Unusual ability; excellent work.
Art: Has real talent and should continue to study.
Crafts: Always has a definite plan and carries it out.

The grade equivalent scores for the Iowa Basic Skills tests showed Reading and Arithmetic totals both 11th grade; Work Study Skills, and Language Skills totals both 10th grade.

This sensitive and talented girl had difficulty in relating to other people. When she found there was no point in competition and when she didn't have to prove her superiority she relaxed and became warm toward others. Her independence was a marvelous quality that all the teachers valued; they were glad when she made genuine social progress without losing her independence.

Here is an entering six-year-old's report in first grade:

Physical State: Barnes has plenty of energy, never seems to be tired; has a large appetite. The need for frequent drinks and toileting at the beginning of the year has disappeared. He can rest well, but more than half the time, is noisy, demanding attention.
Social State: He is very anxious to be loved and accepted by the group but cannot bring himself for long to play any but rough games. Of these the other boys soon tire, and although they have tried to pull him into other types of play, they do not succeed for long. He has frequently to be removed from the group, because he gets too

rough and bodily damage does result. He has accepted some responsibility for the care of the guinea pigs, but will not always carry it
out. He loves them, but his own needs are so pressing he cannot put
them aside for needs of guinea pigs. He enjoys group games, but
finds it very hard to wait his turn.

Emotional Stability: He is emotionally unstable, potential dyna-
mite in a group. When getting individual attention he can carry along
very well, and at his present stage it seems the only way for him to
learn. He reacts very unhappily to failure, feels miserable if his
paper becomes torn or mussed. He is conscious of this and tries to
work carefully. He is sincere and straight forward. He does not
respect others' property and is very possessive of his own things.
He scatters his belongings about and always needs help in gathering
them when he goes home.

Work Habits: He is interested and curious, observes important
things on trips. When his interest is captured he can listen to directions and follow them. He becomes easily angered at himself and at
situations. With firmness on our part he is gaining a modicum of
self-control which is sometimes startling in the suddenness with
which it appears. He loves the music period and cooperates there
each day better than at any other time. He tries everything and is
improving in the use of his body. He enjoys singing and wants to
enter into dramatics, but his lack of control frequently spoils his
participation.

Reading: He reads very well and is just now at a point where he
responds very well to instruction which we are giving to him *alone*.
He enters into some reading activities but is advanced beyond most
of the group. Reading may be an emotional stabilizer for him, since
it is a quiet activity in which he is not stimulated by other children.
In this, as in everything, he demands so much individual attention,
that he is a problem to our routine. His oral vocabulary may be
very good, but he has difficulty expressing himself with clear enun-
ciation or with logical sequence. The assistant and I are having
frequent chats with him in private to help him express himself.

Shop: He works hard, but does not consider other people's rights.

Art: Disturbing in class, though he has obvious talent. He is care-
less with his paints, noisy, bumps into other children.

Science: He works hard in digging, collecting, carting in wheelbarrows, etc. but again, wanting to be first, refuses to obey instruc-
tions, spoils his opportunity to learn or to have a good time.

Barnes seems to have the stuff of success if he can learn self control, patience, emotional poise, respect for the rights of others, in
other words, grow in emotional maturity up to the level of his mental
development.

Because the parents agreed to work with us and with outside con-
sultants, we kept Barnes, and here is the fourth grade report (first
semester):

Physical State: Barnes is in good health; the fact that he is over-
weight does not seem to keep him from being very active. His rest
has been improving steadily and he seems to be more relaxed.

Social Relationships: We are currently in an era of good feeling,
and qualities of giving and understanding which are to be found in
Barnes' personality are magnificent to behold. There are ups and

105

downs, of course, but Barnes is trying very hard to learn how to get along with other people. He can help, defer to, symphathize with, and make allowances for others in a really unselfish way when he is feeling good about himself. He can sense what other people need for encouragement and, when not involved in his own troubles, can supply this with little self-consciousness. He is becoming more sure of his position in the group and the children have begun to realize the value of his friendship. His frustration level is still terrifically low, which of course is a handicap in getting along with others as well as himself.

Emotional Stability: Barnes is developing a kind of equilibrium which he has lacked. He can sometimes concentrate on his work. He responds very well to approval and warmth from others, and is building a core of self-approval based on a more realistic appraisal of himself. He still has a tendency to react in extremes, to try to get his own way by violent displays of love or anger. It will be some time, of course, before he can withstand much frustration. He needs the reassurance of adult guidance.

Curriculum: During the course of our study on China, Barnes has been increasingly able to operate under his own steam and to evaluate his work in a more critical manner without being discouraged. He has a tremendous amount of curiosity and enthusiasm which will be more and more useful to him as he develops perseverance and good work habits. His school work is greatly dependent upon his emotional state and he needs much encouragement to keep him going.

In the Iowa Basic Skills tests Barnes ranked normal for his age. He has been surging ahead in arithmetic, motivated more by competition than is healthy. He needs to calm down and develop more thoroughness; but he is learning a great deal. He loves to read and he profits from his reading. His stories are affected more by lack of concentration than by lack of imagination, so that those he finishes are good. His writing has been improving.

So, by slow stages (and it always takes longer than you think) Barnes built enough self-confidence and self-control to begin enjoying work. He was an example of the fact that growth is never even; but once started feeling good about himself, he relapsed into old patterns less often, and for shorter periods each time.

Reports on and from Alumni

Every generation of Rose Valley parents has wanted to know how their children would manage the transition to another school. Will they be prepared? Will they be able to adjust to formal and rigid routines characteristic of so many schools? Will they succeed? We wanted to know that, too, for if they did not make it, our school's survival would be in question. We expected them to have difficulty accepting the values and practices of conventional schools. After all, The School in Rose Valley was made out of parents' rebellion to those same practices. We sent out questionnaires to seventh grade teachers in schools where our pupils had transferred and to the children themselves. We asked what was wrong in their background and what was right. A few children indicated mathematics and grammar as difficult subjects, but said they were ahead in social studies, in science, and in the arts. Teachers reported that in the areas where they were weak their attitude about learning was exceptionally good; the children were resourceful, responsible, independent workers and, thus, valuable additions to the school.

One boy, talking over what it was like in seventh grade, (they always came back to visit us on holidays) said, "You know, I'm busier this year, but not working as hard as I did here." He deplored "busy work" when there was real work to do. This same boy reported on a later questionnaire: "The fact that I was accustomed to working much closer to the limit of my abilities than was required in high school, of course, made for an easy transition."

Later we added the question: "Would you send your children to a school like this one?"

Responding to the most recent questionnaire (1964), 42 out of 51 of our 1936–56 graduates who responded said they would put their children through the same experience they had enjoyed. Five said, "Maybe"; four said "No." Those in favor stressed the breadth of the program and the emphasis on individual development; those opposed deplored the lack of discipline and drill. A few quotations follow:

1. I honestly believe that my basic education in natural sciences, arts, music, and social studies all stems from Rose Valley. High school added nothing to this base. I would choose a school like this for: the comfortable environment, small classes, woods, individual attention, individual projects possible, and lack of any "busy work."

2. Initiative and curiosity are the two most important things I took away from Rose Valley and I've still got a little left, although practically all of my subsequent education has done its best to kill them. "Study to pass, not learn" is the thesis of American education at all of the levels I've experienced—and it's a very easy thing to do. Too many of my contemporaries have finished with good grades and little education. If I got any more than they did (education, not grades), I think I can honestly attribute it to Rose Valley. As soon as they are old enough my kids will be there.

3. I will do my utmost to secure a Rose Valley type education for my children because I believe it was one of the most important and valuable influences in my formative years. The essence of the Rose Valley contribution is, I feel, that it aids the child in freely developing into his own unique type of human being, rather than training him to fit anonymously into a pre-established pattern. Some of our contemporary literature is concerned with the effects suburban housing developments and large business organizations are having on the individual. A Rose Valley education, is, in part, an answer to this problem, for I cannot imagine a Rose-Valley-ite succumbing entirely to the pressures of conformity.

Another important Rose Valley contribution was the understanding and appreciation it developed in us of nature and natural processes.

As Rose Valley pupils, these people had been thoroughly involved; and you do not forget that kind of experience.

107

13

AN EXPERIMENT IN THE SEARCH FOR COMMITMENT

T HE FOLLOWING LETTER marked the beginning of a two-month experiment by our sixth grade teacher, Ellie Fernald. The experiment was an attempt to overcome a lack of inner motivation and personal involvement on the part of a group of sixth grade pupils. The need for the experiment would not have been felt, and an experiment of this sort certainly would never have been permitted in most schools. Its essence was to eliminate all required activity for a limited period. Early in February 1966, the teacher initiated her experiment by writing the parents of these children:

DEAR SIXTH-GRADE PARENTS:

The present sixth grade is a capable group, capable of "producing" when "producing" is expected. But, there is something missing. That "something" is a sense of personal commitment, and a willingness on the part of each child to meet challenges openly, sincerely, and directly. Motivation for school "work" rarely comes from within the children, and the social forces within the group are working *against* the development of strong individuals. Too many are incapable of involvement at the present time. Too many have become slick and adept in accepting superficiality in themselves and in others. Too many can give quick and meaningless answers, and too many are working either to get finished or to please me. These things have caused the teachers who work with them to try *anything* in the way of teaching devices to bring forth the kinds of responses we would like to see. In some cases, we have seen good things—in writing, in art, in drama, in dance, sometimes in social studies projects. But all too often it takes extreme effort and contrivance (on our part).

Since learning is the exploration and discovery of personal meaning, the learning process itself must be a highly personal one. Because the class is small, it would be quite possible to allow for and promote this kind of individual interest and growth. But for many long-standing reasons, the children themselves fight against it. There is a great deal of hiding in this group; it has become very easy for them to find immediate protection in numbers, or to

108

find immediate protection in going through the motions of "doing something the teacher wants you to do." Rarely have they been forced to direct themselves, to set their own goals, in short, to find out what it is to be truly an individual.

We have asked ourselves how. How can we get them to come to grips with their school experience in a lasting and real way?

On occasion, we have set aside blocks of time in which no specific tasks are required of the children. Because of habit and the scheduling of special subjects, we have spent only isolated mornings or afternoons with this atmosphere. Some of this time has been used well by some, and productive ideas, interests, projects have developed at these times. Others, and it seems to be a majority, are not yet able to set themselves in motion on a self-appointed task, and they become restless, bored, angry. But they have always known that tomorrow, things will be back to normal. None, of course, can verbalize this. It's not something of which they are conscious. But as an experiment, we now are watching to see what happens if there is *no* time limitation (therefore no escape); we are prepared to continue a non-scheduled approach for as long a period of time as it takes for this group to "come to." We are supportive of any signs of personal involvement, feeling that the recognition of one's individual interests and limitations, plus commitment to a direction, are the most valuable learnings for the group at this time. It will not be difficult for some; it will be terribly difficult for others. Already, after only two days, there has been a good deal of shiftless boredom and anger, for we have refused to give in to demands for the kinds of tasks that merely serve to keep one busy. We are constantly faced with the question, "Well, what *should* I be doing?" We throw the question back to them. We are available to give support and help when it is sought, but we are not directing the show. It is uncomfortable, but seems to be the only way we can find to make the group itself feel the problem. They have preferred until now to avoid this recognition.

It is important that you know the reasons for all this, and that's why I've tried to set them down. It's also important that we *not* tell the children what's behind it, nor that it won't last forever, they *must* wrestle with it themselves for this to be effective. It may be a week, it may be a month before we are ready to go back to the "normal" curriculum, or before we find the direction so sorely needed. Thank you for your cooperation and understanding. If you'd like a conference at any time during this period, which is bound to be difficult, please give me a call.

Sincerely,
ELLIE

On March 9, 1966, one month after the beginning of this "experiment," a meeting of the parents of the sixth grade was called to report our observations and hunches about the results of our experiment.

The tangibles were easy to point to; the evidence of busy hands was everywhere about us. There was the greenhouse (green, of course) complete with already sprouting seedlings. It was the result of many girl-hours in the shop, and represented the overcoming of several construction disasters—but there it was, beginning to flower. There were the bunk beds, double and even triple, and the small forts and "houses" built in every conceivable part of the room. The beds had been built from discarded canvas cots, originally intended as places to go to read or be alone, later to be used in overnights at the school. There was the huge papier-mâché Egyptian sphinx, masterfully supported by furniture and by strings from the ceiling—a project undertaken by a boy who somehow felt he should be working on something related to what used to be the "curriculum." There was a beautifully carved fifty-pound plaster slab depicting an Assyrian winged creature with five legs. There were models of bridges built from drinking straws, carefully "researched" in a book discovered in the class library. There was a large black and white painted screen of an oriental scene, inspired by an art trip to an impressive Japanese exhibit in Philadelphia. There were tissue paper murals on the windows, and poems on the walls. The poetry, written primarily by the girls, was poured over and revised with great earnestness; they were each other's critics, and they spent a part of nearly each day sharing and discussing their writings. There were recordings of the writing and some extemporaneous speeches on the tape-recorder. Hanging from the ceiling were three-dimensional woven constructions, both delicate and massive, inspired by some experimentation with a science kit on "Space Geometrics."

Just outside the room were wooden catapults built by several of the boys; these had since turned into snowball throwing and ball-pitching machines. Across the field and high in a tree was a tree-house; down the hill and looking very much like a tea-house in the woods was another "fort," built entirely of small branches fastened together with vines. There were several rooms in this intricate construction, and the whole class could be inside it together. There were vows that we would hold classes there in the spring. At the foot of the hill, sadly sunk forever in the creek, was a waterlogged but handsome raft, built and rebuilt by energetic boys who were sure they could take a trip if only the logs wouldn't soak up so much water.

Several members of the class began inviting visitors to come to the sixth grade and speak to us about various topics. First there were letters to authors of some favorite books—questions about the books, invitations to visit, and general comments of appreciation. These were followed by an interest in finding out about various professions. The girls wrote a letter to a local potter, who had previously been a professional modern dancer in New York. He spent the day with us, talking, working with us in clay, dancing with us. The boys were easily drawn into the dancing and seemed comfortable with the kinds of movement he suggested for us to try. And, of course, that day and those following produced many pots and clay creatures which by early March were now crowding our tables and shelves.

There had also been much discussion and wonder about war and peace; members of the class were aware of debate in the adult community about the war in Vietnam, and wanted to know why some strongly opposed the war. We invited a youth worker from the Friends' Peace Committee in Philadelphia to explain his views, and we spent a very profitable afternoon of discussion with him. He happened to bring up the topic of refugees, and this captured the attention of the class. Suddenly we found ourselves wanting to "do something" to help refugees. Someone suggested raising money to send to refugees in another country. Others wanted to make something that refugees might find useful. We wrestled with various possibilities, and within a few days we found ourselves weaving a blanket. It was perhaps the most exciting thing that happened during the month, because it pulled the class together in a way that nothing had before. We wove two by two squares on simple cardboard looms, with fragments of yarn from a myriad of sources; we sat for days on our small rug on the floor. We were eager about what should have been a monotonous task, but wasn't. For some reason the rug was made primarily by the boys. They threw themselves into the job, carrying their looms with them all over school, working at home, involving little brothers and sisters and even mothers in the job. Our blanket grew, and it was magnificent. Every square was different, and the final effect was dazzling. We spent many long moments of admiration when we finally saw it hanging on the wall.

The next question, of course, was "who are we going to send it to?" We sent out another invitation—this time to a member of the American Friends' Service Committee (AFSC) who had recently been in Jordan, Algeria, and the Congo. He showed us slides and spoke of his experiences, giving us the flavor of the three areas, with particular reference to the refugee situations. We debated and debated about our blanket; it certainly couldn't do much good because there were so many refugees. After all, it was only one blanket. Perhaps we could sell our blanket, and use the money to purchase something that could do more good for more people. Our latest visitor had stressed the idea of "self-help," a concept the class found intriguing. What could we send that would go along with this idea? One of the slides we had seen showed a group of women refugees in Algeria receiving some cotton cloth from AFSC, from which they would make their families' clothes. Perhaps we could send some fabrics for women to use in this way, for, after all, everyone needs clothing. How much material could we afford to buy with the money we hoped to raise from the sale of our blanket? How were we going to sell the blanket? Again, there was much debate, because the blanket was important to everyone. The decision was reached that it would be sold in a kind of secret auction in which everyone in school, parents included, could contribute to the "purchase"; the blanket itself would be given as a farewell present to Grace Rotzel, who was retiring at the end of the year. No one could predict how

111

much money we might raise in this way; we were thrilled when the actual total came to something over one hundred dollars. We were even more thrilled when we went to the mill outlet to buy our fabrics, and both boys and girls spent several excited hours choosing bold and beautiful pieces of cotton. The one hundred dollars bought so much material that we almost couldn't fit in the car to go back to school.

(We lived proudly with our materals for some time before they actually left for Algeria; we lived with our blanket until June, at which time it was presented to Grace with great ceremony.)

What else happened during the month of the "experiment?" We gave a French play; some individuals did some reading; the girls worked as "assistants" in the Five's group and in the shop; several of the boys did some demonstration dissections with the preschool; we printed a newspaper written by the first grade; we worked with the first-graders in recording their stories both on the tape recorder and on paper. We played guitars nearly every day; all but two of the children expressed a desire to learn how to play, and one by one, they begged and borrowed a motley collection of instruments which gradually assumed great importance in the class. We sang both as individuals and as a group; we learned much by inviting guitarists and banjoists to join us. And when we went about the school, we began to hear other guitars and familiar songs and began to see other bunk beds and forts and woven squares. And we were proud.

These were specific things we could point to, at the meeting of the parents in March. There were other things, too, but they were less tangible.

What had happened to the group when all the artificial supports of "schedule" and structured curriculum were pulled out from under them? There had been, at first, the anger and jitteriness we had expected. There was much running, semi-serious wrestling, shiftlessness. There was no easy way to help the class understand *why* this was happening to them either; this made it even more difficult at first. But little by little, the group settled into a slower, calmer, more natural state, so that after about two weeks, there was a more or less even flow to the school day. There was no longer the expectation that "a teacher is to tell you what to do." There was no need for a clock in the room; "recesses," rather than rigid half-hours tied to something arbitrary like the clock, became simple "breaks" whenever individuals or small groups felt a need to get outside and run around. Indeed, recesses and even lunch, on occasion, were completely missed if we all happened to forget at the same time.

There were also shifts in the social organization of the group. Some of the less aggressive members of the class were suddenly "discovered" in the less frantic atmosphere, and new associations began to form. There was much less animosity between the boys and girls—even friendly co-operation at times. There was more listening, based on a respect for one another more honest than one imposed by a teacher in ordinary classroom situations.

There was for everyone *at least once* a feeling of pride in having done, made, or built something that the group valued; there was also the beginning of a willingness to examine the quality of accomplishments, rather than doing something for the sake of getting it done. There was a growing strength on the part of individuals to say "go away, I'm busy," where this had been nearly impossible in the group before.

At times deep concern was expressed about the things we were *not* doing in areas such as science, math, and social studies. There were fears about whether they would be "behind" when they went on to seventh grade. These comments were usually followed, however, by others expressing a desire to retain as much as we could during the remainder of the year of the feeling and atmosphere of these weeks.

The reinstating of "academic" subjects and a modified schedule came about as a result of some heated class meetings. Spring vacation was approaching, and the general feeling of the children was that we should return to "normal" after that week-long break. The proposed schedule was a masterpiece of compromises; it was a schedule in which we tried to operate as flexibly as possible. It was a schedule in which large blocks of free time were built in and guaranteed.

The situation following vacation may have seemed proper and normal to the children, but it certainly had a different quality about it for those of us who worked with the group. We were again going through the routines of teaching and learning within a more formal classroom structure, but the attitude of the class was different. The problems hadn't disappeared completely; but the major obstacles had been tempered, and there was an openness and enthusiasm that we had been trying to reach earlier in the year.

As an attempt to draw from the parents of the sixth-graders more than had come out at our meeting in March, we sent to each home a questionnaire that asked for rather lengthy replies. The response was somewhat less than satisfactory, because few were actually completed and returned. Those we did receive were helpful with respect to individual children; most helpful however, was the generous parent-support and trust during the actual experiment. There was a genuine spirit of co-operation from the parents; their patience helped to make this a worth-while experience for all of us.

ELLIE FERNALD

During this experiment, the staff brought up the inevitable question: Why had these children, brought up in a school that believed in the satisfaction of work for work's sake, reached the sixth grade with so little of that satisfaction? Had we made them too dependent on requirements? Had there been too much direction? Obviously, for this group, unlike most previous sixth grades, there had been something missing between our beliefs and our practice. We knew from experience that genuine education that develops inner discipline comes from self-direction. Every child must be trained, but his development into a man or a woman depends on far more than training. From babyhood, if he grows normally, he must have choices. The strong protective fence of rules and regulations, provided by adults, must be pushed back a little farther each year if he is to develop his own unique qualities and interests. He must have a chance to fail and succeed, to grow in trust in himself until he can stand alone and not feel insecure. If he has had training and freedom in the right proportion, by eleven years of age he should be started on the process of his own education that will continue through life.

This experiment helped the children to trust themselves. Their teacher had the nerve to risk their alarm and anger at being thrown back on themselves and the strength to carry through. This is never easy.

The appended graph, giving the group norm on the May Basic Skills Test of that year, shows that, far from being behind, as these children had feared, they had made normal gains academically. Taking time for this experiment hadn't penalized them; the experience had increased their will to learn.

IOWA TESTS OF BASIC SKILLS

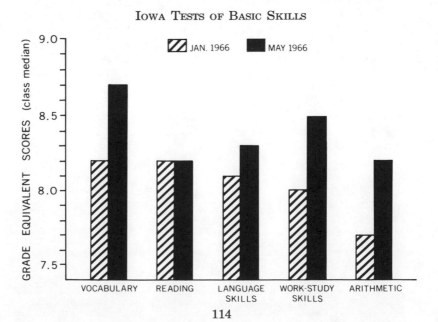

14

A STAFF STUDY OF SEX AND EMOTIONAL MATURITY

I N A SMALL SCHOOL like ours, in an atmosphere of openness and acceptance, one gets to know intimately the ups and downs of the young. In 1948 there was a period of rather troubling sexual problems which seemed to call for more wisdom than any of us had, and I sought our Dr. Leon Saul with a plea for help. A psychiatrist of unusual caliber, he had recently moved to the community, had put his children in our school, and had indicated his interest in helping this venture in education.

When I told Dr. Saul about this problem, he listened sympathetically, suggested that we sit down with the staff and discuss sexuality in relation to a child's development, and after that discuss the emotional development of the child from conception to three years, in a series of staff meetings. Thus we began a study that continued through 1955 with benefit to the whole school. It changed us all.

Fortunately we had the habit of free discussion, but even so, the notes on those early meetings show that tension and strain permeated them, for we were more or less an average group with our own inner fears and wariness of new ideas; besides, a discussion of sex is not handled with the same aplomb by teachers as a discussion of arithmetic. We started with varying degrees of willingness, one teacher commenting that she felt problems of the emotions were best solved by religion.

The summary of these meetings shows where we needed the clarification. That children's sexual feelings change in intensity we knew, and that they must be domesticated was obvious, but since this was largely a home problem, what could a school do? The answer, Dr. Saul said, was—"Understand."

"Part of the difficulty in dealing with sex problems," he explained, "lies in the phenomenon itself; the other part lies in ourselves. We must avoid being emotional and seek to be objective."

Since sexual aberrations often express hostility of some sort, the question arose, how much hostility is normal. Isn't it normal for a child to be born not satisfied, and to strive for satisfaction? Isn't it normal for him to buck up against taboos in the process of domestication, and isn't this bound to come out as hostility? Gradually some answers emerged. Hostility is a fundamental biological force in the personality, useful for self-preservation, and also one of the most difficult to domesticate. The happy healthy child can handle the normal hostilities derived from the arrival of a sibling, or from being weak, small, and dependent, or from being excluded at times; but when he shows persistent fears or hostility, something is wrong. What we need to keep in mind is that sexual feelings, beginning in the three-to-seven-year period, are stronger than most of us realize, and the child's efforts to cope with them must be respected; that these basic impulses are so strong and the ego so weak that appropriate, externally imposed checks are necessary for the development and socialization of sex.

Adult (parent and teacher) application of those "good checks" can be so restrictive, due to our own unrecognized anger, that we can contribute to the hostility already generated in the child. In addition to this, Dr. Saul pointed out that we should keep in mind two aspects of sexuality: sex as a biologic force, and sex as a pathway for the expression and drainage of emotional impulses and tensions. The child who is masturbating may be telling you that other active outlets for his energy have been denied him; or he may be protesting a too rigid and impersonal home atmosphere that is keeping him dependent, inhibited, and feeling inferior. Sexual growth toward freedom and independence is bound to have ups and downs; all children have emotional problems. The goal of education is not therapy but understanding; it is necessary for both pupils and teachers to learn not only about the differences in people but also about the differences between the normal and the pathological. The divergence here is in degree only, and nobody, not even the so-called "normal" child, is normal all the time.

We needed to know the risks involved in complete freedom, as well as in too much repression. Real objectivity was impossible, but we tried to become aware of our own responses and separate them from the problems we were meeting in children. The main issue, it became clear, was the parents' (and teachers') appreciation of the delicacy of feelings and sensitivity of the twig to being bent. It is dangerous to tamper with a child's small ego; adults should have complete sympathy with the child's feelings and impulses, and a tolerance of his behavior, and also be able to give sympathetic discouragement to inappropriate overt sexual expression. Thus it was

116

our job to develop, and to help parents develop, a way to socialization without "antagonization."

The monthly meetings began to be bi-monthly, for our interest was aroused in Dr. Saul's suggestion that we try to find out what made a healthy child, instead of focusing on problems. He said a great deal of research had been done, and much published on the abnormal child, but comparatively little on the signs and bases of emotional health in children. Confusions in our concepts of what was normal came up frequently. For example, someone quoted Dr. Gesell as saying that all children retreat for about six months around the age of two, or two and one-half, and that, therefore, shyness was not a symptom but a norm.[1] Another quoted the same source as reporting that nightmares were normal to six-year-olds. Dr. Saul cautioned us that even if this were true for the children of the Gesell series, it merely indicated that this was the normal average for the group studied, not that it is ideal or unavoidable under different circumstances or controls.

Our study kept pulling us into deeper involvement with emotional maturity. Since we were urged to make our own rating scales, we were constantly probing our own values. We began by making an outline for our notes on individual pupils, with such headings as *Attitude toward Adults, Toward Children, Toward Himself, Physical Needs, Psychological Needs,* and *Studies.* Then we turned to a negative approach, which seemed easier, and made a list of children's deviations from the normal, such as *Temper Tantrums, Withdrawal,* and *Over-dependence.* We ended with seventeen traits by which we rated all children on a scale from 1 (fewest deviations) to 5 (most deviations). The result showed many variations, due to different interpretations by different teachers. It also showed too little objectivity, and we decided we were too limited by the rigid framework of static and negative qualities we had set up.

In 1951 a psychologist from Swarthmore College took over the leadership of our discussions, and both Dr. Saul and Dr. James Delano (a child psychiatrist who had joined us the previous year) attended many of the meetings. We wrote our own definitions of an emotionally healthy adult, and of the emotionally healthy child of the age with which we were most familiar. We finally combined the results of our thinking under three main headings: *Relationship to Others; Attitude about Self; Attitude toward Living.* When this was done we were asked to make a quick snap-judgment rating of all the children from 1 (closest to normal ideal) to 5 (least healthy). Each was rated by at least three teachers. While there were discrepancies in our ratings, there was more agreement than on our "deviations" ratings. Finally, that year we rated the children on

[1] *Infant and Child in Culture of Today* (Harper, 1943).

117

some of the already existing scales (Merrill-Palmer, Joel, Haggerty, Conrad). We found objections to all of them; but in the process learned to evaluate different types of behavior more objectively.

In 1952 our psychologist moved away. Now Dr. Delano took charge, assisted by another member of the Swarthmore Psychology Department. On the basis of ratings made and of agreement among the staff we selected from each age group one child who most nearly approached the normal ideal. Later we added a second child. Extensive anecdotal notes were taken on these children by group and special teachers, visiting college students, and other observers, and background material on each child was collected.

By this time we were far enough along to find Dr. Saul's book *Emotional Maturity* [2] useful. For the next two years while we collected anecdotal material on pupils, we read and discussed this book that delineates emotional forces in the development of personality. We began to realize the importance of facing our own emotions honestly, the necessity of ferreting out which reactions derived from our own emotions and inner conflicts and which from the circumstances of the moment. Emotions are a part of us, as necessary as the stomach or the lungs, and as capable of producing disease if not properly developed. It isn't possible to deny the hostility in all of us, but it is quite possible to find out something of its sources in each, why it is repressed in some and so free in others, why some of us are inhibited and some are violence-prone and what emotions can do to relationships between children and adults. It is necessary to conform to the social mores of our culture, but it is our privilege and duty to question these mores and their effect on the growing personality. It is possible to discover where our senses of inferiority, superiority, and competitiveness come from, and how to deal with them. We knew about the child's dependency and need for love; what we needed help with was how to guide that dependency toward independence and how to help the child give as well as take.

So, as we discussed anecdotal material, uncomfortable questions arose. We asked, Why I do dislike some children, and how am I to meet their needs? Why is it that when Johnny does such-and-such, it doesn't bother me at all, but when Susie does the same thing I hit the ceiling? Why is it that we accept a girl as a tom-boy, but if a boy of the same age wants to play with dolls, he is a disgrace to the family? Why is it that some children take failure in stride and others are thrown by it? (And the inevitable inner suggestion, How do I take failure?) In the process of searching for answers we learned a bit more of the meaning of acceptance. Dislike is no sin, and it doesn't need to block relationships. Two teachers working with the same children, and having different likes and dislikes,

---

[2] Leon Saul, *Emotional Maturity* (Lippincott, 1947).

118

worked out a plan whereby Susie's actions that caused antagonism
in one teacher, were disciplined by the teacher who was not annoyed.
And, as one teacher remarked, "Just talking about annoyances
helped. I still tie three-year-old Jimmie's shoes sixteen times a
day, but somehow I am not annoyed any more." Each of us was
examining his own guilts, frustrations, inferiority, competitiveness,
and as we moved an inch or two toward self-acceptance, we learned
how to help the children accept themselves.

In 1955 two of us attended a conference at Goddard College on
the role of self-knowledge in the educative process, sponsored by
Drs. Brock Chisholm and Lawrence S. Kubie, which was a culmina-
tion of that for which we had been reaching. It was rewarding and
supportive to know that we were not alone; many teachers were
working on the same idea that Dr. Saul had led us to explore.
During that year Dr. Kubie's commencement address at Goddard
College, "The Forgotten Man of Education," was printed in the
Harvard Alumni Bulletin, and thereafter read and discussed many
times at The School in Rose Valley. Dr. Kubie begins:

Every discipline has its tools, and each tool has its own inherent
errors. Within its own field each discipline is meticulously self-
critical about the sources of error which reside in its special
instruments.

Yet there is one instrument which every discipline uses without
checking its errors, tacitly assuming that the instrument is error-
free. This, of course, is the human psychological apparatus. As a
result of the failure to consider the sources of error in the human
being himself, when our academic disciplines assemble together in
our great educational institutions they reenforce the tacit, fallacious
assumption that man can understand the world that lies outside of
himself. Actually, each man is his own microscope with his own
idiosyncrasies, to which he alone can penetrate. Therefore we cannot perceive the outside world without distorting our very percep-
tions unless we search out individually the sources of error which
lie hidden within. . . . Yet such self-knowledge, which requires the
mastery of intricate new tools of psychological exploration, is wholly
overlooked throughout the entire scheme of "modern" education,
from the kindergarten to the highest levels of academic training.
. . . It is we, the educated and the educators, who have failed mankind, not mankind which has failed us. Science and art and philosophy and religion and learning have failed. . . . The next goal of
education is nothing less than a progressive freeing of man—not
merely from external tyrannies of nature and of other men, but
from internal enslavement by his own unconscious automatic mecha-
nisms.

And he ends:

Without self-knowledge in depth, we can have dreams but not
art, we can have the neurotic raw material of literature, but not
mature literature. Without it we have no adults, but only aging
children armed with words, paints, clay, and atomic weapons, none

119

of which they understand. It is this which makes a mockery of the pretentious claims of education, of the arts, of religion, and of science. Self-knowledge is The Forgotten Man of our entire educational system and indeed of human culture in general.

So it was, that, starting on a search for understanding of sexuality, just one of the emotional forces in a personality, we went on to experiences leading to a beginning of self-knowledge, and thus to a little deeper understanding of what education is all about.

15

PARENTS' ROLES IN THE SCHOOL

CIRCUMSTANCES DICTATED THAT The School in Rose Valley be a do-it-yourself project. New educational ideas were sufficiently different from the old to make it necessary for parents to work with teachers in order to understand what was going on. Democracy within the school, an underlying tenet of progressive education, required an organization of parents, children, and teachers that would permit them all to share various areas of responsibility. And then the depression, born the year the school was begun, created financial conditions that challenged our ability to make do, make over, make out. All of us found it necessary to learn by doing.

Constructing the buildings that we were going to work in was the most spectacular of the parents' work, the most fun, and the most demanding of patience and skill. Mr. Rawson and the children started the building habit, and it has lasted throughout the school's history. They began by putting up "The Mushroom." It was a classroom that was used for four years. But making the Main Building was something quite different. The project lasted from March until September, and then week-ends into the winter. It meant many hours of hard work from mothers, fathers, and children. Most of them, as they went along, learned from the fathers who could direct. This was a determined group of parents. The disillusioning years after the "war to end war" had given them the will to try for a better world and to live from the inside out. It was a large order, to flesh out the bones of Dewey's and Freud's philosophy and what better way to begin than to make the building in which we were to work. The Main Building was made with faith and determination, and, when completed, the most obvious emotion was astonishment. The building was big, with four classrooms, kitchen, library, shop, science room, and four toilets. Made to last ten years, it still functions at the end of forty. Its making must be included under "survival," because it was this kind of cooperation from the parents that was the foundation of the school.

The next big project was to re-establish a location and a program for the youngest children. The experiment from 1933–37, when the nursery school had been a foster child made to earn its own way on a separate budget, had made it increasingly obvious that the nursery school actually was one of the most important parts of the whole structure, for the parents of the youngest children were the most eager to be educated. Hence the Board took an important step when it authorized the addition of a room to make possible a nursery school on the premises.

The debt on the Main Building was no sooner paid than another fund was started. The Admissions and Property committees began intensive work, while the Finance Committee discovered the Whitney Foundation, that, in turn, investigated us. It was comforting to have one of its visitors describe our so simple buildings and apple trees as the most perfect educational set-up she had ever seen, and very restorative of morale to receive a gift of $1,000, which arrived in time to make up a deficiency in a December payroll.

The additional room that been decided upon remained nebulous for some time, and then, one evening in April 1937, it was Owen Stephens' humorous enthusiasm as he showed drawings of a proposed addition to "The Chip" (the rebuilt "Mushroom"), that persuaded us to get to work. The parents now had confidence, and besides, this addition was only to be one room, so there was no difficulty in accepting the plan. The Building Committee worked hard during the summer; approximately six men did the work. On the night before school opened, the last piece of celotex was nailed into place. The October *Bulletin* reported: "The big many-windowed room with brick fireplace, now occupied by four- and five-year-olds is free in the afternoon for folk dancing, rhythms, clay modeling, or any other purpose we choose, and is already proving an asset to every group."

In the thirties, parents busied themselves with other activities than building: a drama workshop produced several one-act plays of Glaspell, Barrie, Yeats, and Shaw; there was an afternoon art class for adults; our English folk dancers regularly used the rhythms of Parson's Farewell, Newcastle, Nonesuch, etc., and danced with the children at school parties; and the apprentice class, a group working with children while they were studying growth and development, had many parent members, as well as graduate students from Vassar and Bennington who were preparing to teach.

In 1940 a Future-of-the-School Committee was appointed. It began to consider adding two more years to the school program, and finally we decided to have a seventh and eighth grade group.

Early in the spring of 1941, work was begun on the addition of four rooms—two floors—with kitchen and dining room. Now the children were old enough to take more responsibility. They cut down an apple tree that was in the way of the builders. (If you have ever watched children getting into the earth with shovels, you sense that digging has an unusual fascination for them.) The parents, as usual, acted as carpenters and bricklayers, and the work took a year and one-half of week-ends to complete. The children, with Mr. Rawson, helped to build the room they first occupied in 1942.

In 1950 the school was again under financial strain. In 1948 we discontinued the two upper grades for lack of facilities and energy, as well as space. The parents were raising money to pave the lane, which was a slough of mud, ruts, and deep holes. They were asking for contributions to equal "the cost of replacing one rear spring on your present car." The children were building. The Nines and Tens had made the "Hut" at the edge of the woods, a building for over-night camping. It had four six-foot bunks and four four-foot ones, a water-proof roof, and a brick and cement fireplace just outside the door. A group of Sixes and Sevens contracted with local architects for plans for a playhouse under the apple tree by the lane. I mentioned, in the hearing of children, the need for a root cellar, and before I knew it they had dug a hole five feet deep!

We needed a major, new preschool building. Some of us doubted

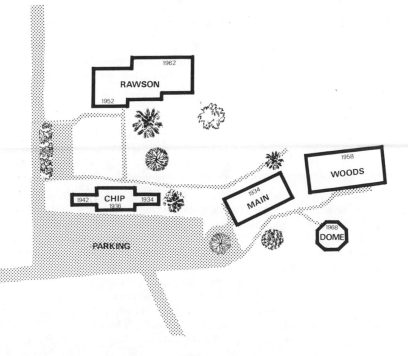

whether there was enough energy and know-how in the parent body at this time to put up an entire building, but John Dickey said, "Let's find out. If there isn't, there won't be one," and he went to work on a most ambitious plan, which required much deliberation. Not until June 1952 did the parents vote unanimously to begin work on one room of the preschool building. Once they got started, it was obvious that the know-how was there, as well as the enthusiasm. Unusual contributions such as steel girders—which permitted the spacious ceiling and clerestory lighting—the herculite for the big windows, joists, roofing, electrical equipment, paint, sinks, acoustic tile, lumber, all made possible an attractive room. The volunteer, unskilled, weekend labor that kept at the work for two years, made the building a structural triumph. It seemed only befitting to name it for Mr. Rawson, the man who had demonstrated the do-it-yourself ideal for eighteen years.

When the Rawson Building was completed, in December 1954, Lin Wolfe wrote an article on "The Great Week-end Project."

We have a unique building in my judgment, . . . fresh in design, functional and tremendously imaginative in the manner in which light, heat, and fresh air are provided. . . . But beyond this I am concerned with a basic speculation: Do we know what we make when we make it?

I am sure of the answer when I think of those few who have been fortunate enough to work together these week-ends. We needed more space to carry on the business of learning, and in the job of creating this space we found ourselves unexpectedly in a learning experience analogous to that of our children in the school. For learning in our school means many things. It is how to cooperate with and enjoy our fellows; it is how to expand leisure time into creative time; it is to know better how to use our personal traits and abilities; it is how to appreciate the creations of others. These are only a few of the goals of learning but all are accessible to both children and parents at The School in Rose Valley.

When, in 1958, it came time for the next building program the Finance Committee, under the leadership of William Brown, thought we could afford to have a contractor. This was unheard of, but the parents welcomed the idea and managed to raise nineteen thousand dollars to make it possible. Woods, the fourth large three-classroom building, was put up in one summer without parental aching backs or sore thumbs. Four years later, it happened again. In 1962, the final two rooms of Rawson, planned when the first room was built in the early fifties, was added one summer by a contractor, thus finishing a complete preschool unit. Now, in 1968–69, the parents have again erected a building, a geodesic dome, hiring a contractor only to lay the concrete floor.

Parents gave more than physical labor. When the men decided to put on a play, we were astonished and delighted with their

124

versatility and hilarious humor. James Skelton wrote the comedy *Psst Hamlet,* directed it, and acted the title role, ably assisted by eight actors; Robert Grooters directed the Danish Pastry Chorus that sang between the acts. Produced in the Media High School, it netted a good sum for the building fund as well as fun for the audience. There were other methods of fund-raising: a Christmas Bazaar, Ice Follies, Merchandise Club, Hedgerow Benefit, May Fair, sales of Christmas trees, magazines, baked goods, a rummage sale, and so on.

Fairs and "putter days" were special occasions when parents enjoyed themselves while contributing to the school. The Christmas Fair started as a holiday party with singing and English dancing; later the annual display of children's books was added, and finally it included a sale of home-made presents, still retaining a family flavor. The May Fair began as a parent effort to help the children who had taken on part of the support of a flooded school in Holland. This, combined with the spring festival with sword and May-pole dancing on the green, also became a time for selling products of children and parents, ending with dinner and square dancing in the evening.

Putter days, two or three Saturdays in the fall, and again in the spring, were also family days when parents and older children took on maintenance jobs such as painting, repairing, landscaping, or whatever else had to be done. The brick terrace at the entrance, and the walks connecting all of the buildings were laid by parents over a period of many putter days. Of course, financial necessity was one big reason for these activities, but there was another—the value of working together for a common goal. One parent said as he was moving away, "I am sorry to go. I have had the value of all I have paid in tuition for my children, in what I myself have learned here. I wouldn't have missed it for anything."

This school would not have been possible without parent co-operation, for the home, the hub of stability for the child, must work in unison with the school if there is to be a healthy learning atmosphere. Fortunately, in the beginning years, many parents wanted to work at the school; the word got around that they were welcome, and we got the habit of expecting them. We asked, "What can you do? How much time can you spend? Can you join the Apprentice Class? When can you start?" The new parent usually started anywhere there was a need, in the kitchen, library, as a bus rider, as henhouse inspector and cleaner, as assistant teacher, as housekeeper—eventually finding a niche that fitted. Many stayed on in important positions, others, when their children left, went on into work in community schools. But always the parents have been unusual in that they were not only knowledgeable, but men and women who knew what they wanted and were willing to work for it.

16

A SUMMING UP

APROFESSIONAL LIFETIME—or most of one—spent on the staff of a really experimental school is bound to teach one a good many things.

I learned not to expect to arrive at a given point, for we never did. To be sure, we had goals that seemed to assume an end, and we made headway toward them; but we came to realize that the accomplishments and the problems that were solved were not important; they were not permanent; it was the *accomplishing* and the *solving* of the problems that showed us how to continue.

We never believed that education was just a "preparation for life," but we were too busy living to indulge in bickering about definitions. When everybody was going full steam, the process was bound to be messy. Animals, a shop, raw materials, gardens, useful junk, collections from stream and woods meant clutter, and clutter was sure to worry somebody. I was bothered sometimes, myself, and said so; but then I was likely to bring in a new set of animals, or something else that increased the clutter.

I could take the physical jumble easier than the mental confusions arising from conflicting ideas. For example, parents who had the preparation-for-life idea of education were concerned that their children were living too much in the present. Wandering by streams was not preparing them for the next grade, or the next school, if they had to move. Would they be ready? I couldn't say. I remember having cold chills myself when we decided to postpone the teaching of reading until the seven-year-old year, but we went ahead anyway. It worked, because we all were enthusiastic; but years later when we decided to return to teaching reading in the first grade, that worked, too. That was the way it was. Policy decisions were always debated and made in the Education Committee (parents and teachers) so I never felt alone.

From the first we realized that a school cannot meet all needs. Our school, based on Dewey's idea that education proceeds in a social environment where children come into contact with their natural surroundings, attracted people who trusted that process. Those who felt uncomfortable with Dewey's concept stayed away, and even deplored us. Growth in enrollment was very slow; it took 36 years to reach the maximum of 150. This was partly because we expected so much of parents—we looked for both faith and works— and partly because we worked hard to make clear our concept of the school in relationship with the child, and generally only those families whose aims were similar to ours were admitted, though there were exceptions.

We were trying to put into action what Dewey meant by the social function of a school. We never educate directly, he said, but indirectly by means of the environment. A child learns from the other children and from the materials he works with, and he finds ways of taking part in what is going on. By small steps he discovers what he can do, and then shares in the activity until he can feel that the group's success or failure is his. This meant children behaving like children and teachers not always teaching, but sometimes learning.

Because of our interest in problem-solving our classrooms looked different from traditional ones; so a common criticism of the school was that there was a lack of discipline. This was understandable. Here was a group deciding whether they should have muslin stage curtains and who should dye them; another was painting a map on the floor and making a mess of it; another was finding out why Italy has gone into Ethiopia, and being very vocal. Because visitors were often confused we limited their number so that we could find time to explain, in terms of our aims, what was taking place; but this did not stop the criticism.

Another reason for this lack-of-discipline criticism was that although we agreed in the beginning that we were not going to take undisciplined problem children, we sometimes did take a child who had been a problem child and had been turned down by other schools. I suppose it was immodest of us, but we tended to think that we—and especially our children—might succeed where others had failed, and who would take him if we didn't. Then we would permit a trial period; this proved fatal for by that time we liked the child too much to let him go, and he *was* making progress. Often the parents of such children had rebelled so hard against authority that they had deprived their young of the ordinary domestication process necessary for growth. Since these children

127

had had years of developing negative patterns, they couldn't change all at once, which meant considerable chaos at school. They had to have time to find themselves in a different setting; youngsters helped each other in this process and almost all grew in their sensitivity to the needs of others.

Another thing I learned was that self-discipline was the backbone of the educational process. When that was strong, everything else fell into place. I learned to recognize the humming sound of children at work on their own initiative and I knew it for a sign that all was well. Parents wanted the *results* of self-discipline, but were often impatient with the slow process of getting it. We all shared these feelings, but, as a result of our work in child study, we were committed to the slow process, to self-initiated experience, the confusion, the failures, and the gradual growth of self-respect and self-confidence. We found it made a great difference in our thinking if we ourselves were going through the same sort of process we were offering the children. So we had classes for adults in clay, painting, or woodwork, and urged parents and teachers to explore something they knew nothing about—learning Russian, or how to manage a garden. Then they could see for themselves how learning disciplined and how it led on to confidence and joy in work. They could understand the stupidity of using gold stars, marks, blue ribbons, or punishments as incentives, and they could agree that offering such incentives was even immoral, because they were ulterior motives that denied the reward in work for work's sake.

Parents working in the school helped disseminate these ideas of learning and discipline, and gave a family feeling to the place, as did the relationships among the children: sixth-graders tutoring first-graders, fourth-graders helping first-graders build their chicken house by putting on the roof; older children taking dictation from kindergarten story-tellers and news-gatherers; all learning to get along with only a reasonable number of fracases. The whole school sang together every morning, which meant a common bond of songs; children and adults learned the same square dances, and so could dance together. Good feeling about themselves and each other had to be an accompaniment to normal living.

I learned to recognize that where problem-solving was shared, problems were usually opportunities to move ahead. This school, being in the country, needed a curriculum that used the country. In the beginning someone had a vision of a science laboratory, manned by a scientist, somewhere on the school grounds, to which children could go with their questions about bugs, soil, water, plants, and beasts that lived in the woods. In those years a laboratory was completely out of reach. It was better so. Each teacher began to make of her room a little laboratory and to study the immediate environment of orchard and stream. The complete unanimity of

128

the staff on that idea and the drive arising from concerted action resulted eventually in a laboratory and a scientist. It was simple and inexpensive, and most of the apparatus was made by the teacher and the parents.

The first student teachers who began to come to us for training posed many problems. Everyone was handling a full-time job and there seemed to be no time for extras. But gradually the teachers worked out a plan giving everyone a part. Each teacher was responsible for giving student teachers an introduction to the subjects he taught, or to the special age-level with which he was most familiar. One teacher managed the course, which expanded to include parents as well as students. The demands of this course, as well as our need to put down on paper what we were doing and why, resulted in a series of bulletins and magazine articles written by teachers.

Conflicts about our philosophy and our practices were another kind of problem, but they could present opportunities for improvements and re-evaluation. One year the Education Committee exploded because we were not giving enough drill in arithmetic and grammar. They went off to visit other schools with pencils and paper to take down academic requirements and achievements and compare them with those of The School in Rose Valley. Parents who had had a traditional preparation-for-life education rated ability to pass tests as the most important criteria; and, of course, we knew that if our children could not pass tests the school would not survive. I shuddered; hoped for the best; expected the worst. Maybe our children were not academically the equal of their peers. What then! As it happened, the visiting committee found our children were not behind. The atmosphere changed from cold to warm; comparisons were favorable. But more important that that, the interest the committee had developed in the whole curriculum caused them to enlarge their scope, and they spent another month producing a *Curriculum Goals Bulletin* that is still in use. It has six headings:

1. Understanding ourselves.
2. Understanding others.
3. Communication.
4. Orientation in time and space.
5. The physical world.
6. Government and law.

The project solved a conflict, put us ahead in our thinking, and also gave us a better understanding of the teaching-learning process.

And naturally there were emotional problems among the adults as well as among the children. The staff study on emotional maturity helped considerably, because it made us all look at ourselves. That didn't mean that we all became mature, but it eased some of our rigidities. Young teachers who came in during the later fifties and

129

early sixties said we were not carrying out all the concepts in which we believed. This was true, and needed to be said. The experiment in a search for commitment (see chapter 13) was in response to this criticism and showed how one teacher worked on the problem.

The young teachers, in turn, had to learn that children were not little adults, and, because they were children, needed more support from structure than often the young teachers were willing to give. So we talked. And talked again, and kept on talking. There were hurt feelings, but not permanent damage. Some problems got solved; others we learned to live with, and, because everybody cared, we could respect each other's point of view.

I learned the need for boundaries and structure. I found these were especially important for us to demonstrate and explain, for we were a progressive school and suffered from rumors about misguided experiments in permissiveness and from the misunderstandings of critics. We were always struggling to find the fine line between permissiveness and control that the adult must walk if the child is to feel secure and is to mature normally. Each teacher, by failure and success, was continually finding the balance that worked for him.

Basically we believed that the task of the elementary school is to see to it that the child's original enthusiasm is directed toward learning. This means that the school plans experiences for children in which they gain understanding of themselves and others; experiences to gain basic skills and concepts of language, mathematics, history, geography, and science; and participation of children in, and some responsibility for, the school community and the wider community.

Our goals, in general, were to have children acquire an enjoyment of work and to have them approach learning honestly, for its own sake. To attain this, the school used other motives for learning than competition for marks, although it recognized competition as ever present.

Children acquire academic skills as rapidly as possible and each according to his ability, and realize that these are not ends in themselves but tools necessary for what they want to find out. They take responsibility for academic work, chores, social relationships, according to capacity, and in ever increasing degree. A large part of experience is planned in the trying-out, do-it-yourself areas. There should be opportunities to discover; problems that call for use of skills in solving. Examples include finding the meaning of pi, working out a formula, writing and producing a play, making a weekly newspaper and a magazine, making equipment in shop, and carrying out a science experiment.

Opportunities for teacher- and parent-learning were provided by the school, with the staff meeting regularly with a consultant to discuss how to infuse mental health principles into school processes and relationships. Other courses were provided such as creative writing, mathematics, art. As problems of school and home often overlap, parents as well as teachers have had access to counseling through the school, and because everything that happens to a child contributes to his education in one way or another, parents and teachers conferred frequently to understand the influences shaping the child.

One of these influences is the educational structure of the school. Structure has been a difficult word for progressives; it has meant to them rigid programs of unchanging subject matter, a concept they have rejected. However, structure is implicit in the nature of a school, and subject matter, far from having to be unchanging, should reflect the needs of the whole school community. Our curriculum evolved from the basic concepts the teachers agreed were important to this school and for these children; structure would depend partly on teachers and partly on children. We determined the major areas and expected to help the children choose from these areas what they were to work on, and how.

I learned to look for support from others working on problems and ideas that we had in common. Most often this was through books. While we were working on classroom structure, a most important book, *The Dynamics of Learning* by Nathaniel Cantor,[1] gave us many topics for staff discussions. It was the first book we had found that gave a clinical picture of what happened in education when students were asked to make their own structure. Dr. Cantor, a pioneer in this subject, had the nerve to throw his college students back on themselves. He gave them the college requirements for the course, reading lists, etc. and then said, "Make of this what you will. You will discover what you want from this course, and how you propose to get it." And to their questions as to how many books they should read, and how many papers they should write, his answer was, "That is up to you." The reports of class discussions revealed anger and resistance, also self-criticism and self-guidance. We elementary school teachers felt some of the same emotions, but realized that if that process had been started in the elementary school with those students, it might have saved a lot of wasted motion. Dr. Cantor was only one of many authors we read and discussed as we groped toward new ideas.

The Aims of Education, by Alfred North Whitehead,[2] was a valuable book for us in the beginning. It described the three stages of education—romance, precision, generalization—and made clear that a stage of precision is barren without a previous stage of

[1] (Buffalo, N.Y.: Henry Stewart, Inc., 1946.)
[2] (Macmillan, 1929).

romance. Since we were trying to provide the environment for the stage of romance—discovering frogs' eggs, flying kites, etc.—we read and reread his book.

Another book of great interest was *Education through Art* by Sir Herbert Read. He said, "Constructive education only makes sense if it is based on visual, plastic, musical, kinetic, verbal, and symbolic education. That is to say, there is a necessary connection between the validity of thought and the form in which that thought is expressed." This was the kind of education we were groping toward, so it was most satisfying to find this book. Sense perception was important in another work, *Pereceiving, Behaving, Becoming,* the work of a committee of the National Education Association in 1962. This emphasized the growth of a "fully functioning person" and brought us back to Leon Saul's book, *Emotional Maturity,* used in our staff study of 1948–53, where this was defined. In *Teacher,* Sylvia Ashton-Warner seemed to be talking directly to us and with us. She, in this book, led us to Tolstoy and his school.[3]

Recent books such as *Education and Ecstasy* by George Leonard; *The Lives of Children* by George Dennison; *Schools without Failure* by William Glasser; and *Freedom to Learn* by Carl Rogers are taking the shackles off education and pointing toward more freedom to learn.[4]

I learned that in a school there was no need to hurry. Time was too important to waste by hurrying. We could never accept acceleration as a goal. It was subversive of nature. There is an order of development of the nervous system to be respected. It is impossible to cut a year out of a child's life. At four the child's bones, teeth, taste buds, disposition are all four years old and cannot be expected to be six, because his mother wants him to learn to read. "He's bright, and I don't want him to be bored." Neither do we. And if he is bright he needs all the time he has to explore and get started on his own. The growth process is uneven and must have time. The child naturally spurts ahead, slows down, and stands still periodically while growing. If this process is tampered with and forced, there is danger of frayed nerves. This is pulling the child apart to make him over in another more satisfactory design, but it doesn't work, and he will have to return to his normal pace if he is to succeed.

It is difficult to overemphasize the need for time for self-directed activity—that period of "romance" Whitehead talks about. "My point is," he says, "that a block in the assimilation of ideas inevitably arises when a discipline of precision is imposed before a stage of romance has run its course in the growing mind." We took that to mean that we couldn't always control a child's pace. Here we

[3] Read (Pantheon, 1958); Saul (Lippincott, 1947); Ashton-Warner (Simon & Schuster, 1963).
[4] Leonard (Delacorte, Dell, 1968); Dennison (Random House, 1969); Glasser (Harper & Row, 1969); Rogers (Merrill, 1969).

sometimes got into trouble. "Why are you letting my child stand around. He must be taught"; and he was removed from school. We erred on the other side too. Teachers, being teachers, love to direct. I must say there was not as much self-direction as there could have been. But we talked about it, put it in our weekly curriculum reports, and at coffee-time told each other anecdotes about our children's independent activities and competence in solving their problems.

In the preschool the child works on the learning patterns he will continue throughout his life—who he is, how he can cope with himself, other adults, materials, tools, the earth, animals. He must have periods to enjoy and use his environment. This takes time. We were always holding off parents who wanted us to teach more, "to cultivate the mind," as if the mind wasn't working unless it was being force fed. Our answer was, "Take the child on a bug-collecting tour and watch him use his mind. Watch him make a dump-truck in shop. Don't minimize the learning going on. Give him time to BE."

We tried in many ways to keep an easy pace. For some time, due to small enrollment, we had the advantage of having children of two or three ages in one group. This made for continuity and stability, with the older and the younger learning from each other how to lead and how to follow. Then, with larger enrollment we changed to single age groups, assuming it was for the better. It was; the teachers liked the change; but they found in their single age groups as many levels of maturity, or almost as as many, as they had had before. The disadvantage was that a group might remain the same throughout its school life, lacking the challenge of new children each year and the chance to lead on alternate years. As I write, the school is making a change again to multiple age groups and will have three age groups throughout. We never arrive; we change, and the new insights and inspiration accompanying the changes make for growth in learning.

Our idea of an easy pace was clarified when we discovered Dr. Frances Ilg's report on maturity testing as a guide to entrance to preschool. Dr. Ilg, from the Gessell Clinic in New Haven, Connecticut, has proof from thirty-years' experience that one of the main causes of failure in the first grades was immaturity. To have a quotable scientific report to sustain what we had been doing unscientifically for thirty years was a heady experience. We used Dr. Ilg's material for several years, until somebody had another plan. We dropped the tests, but continued to use the idea.

Children who are spurting ahead, and even those who are going slowly, are usually accepted by teachers; it is the ones who need to stand still who are in trouble. We had an unusual example of this in Slocum. Although we did not usually take new children in our fifth grade, we took him because of his need.

The reports told us, and his father told us in front of him, that he was a failure; there was no doubt about it at all. Our fifth grade teachers asked Slocum to make himself at home, watch for a while and enter in when he was ready. Being timid he watched for almost half the year. It was all so strange he couldn't believe what he saw —children working on mathematics and social studies as if they wanted to. That was not for him.

He went to special classes—art, science, crafts, dancing, singing. There he had never failed. Then, very gradually Slocum began to tackle the hated subjects. From February of his first year until the end of the second he worked hard, both at home and with the teacher as tutor. He really knuckled down and drove himself and not only made up what he needed in academic subjects but showed also unusual ability in art and was especially popular with the children. We were fortunate to be able to let this kind of thing happen.

Time was important for teachers too. We needed to have time to get acquainted with each other, with our environment, and with the process of learning. We did a great deal of talking. Almost from the beginning we started having a teachers' house party the second week-end of school (in September) to have a good time as well as to talk about where we were going, and how and why. In February we had another, because we discovered if anyone was likely to let his tensions get the best of him, it was bound to happen in February.

But all the talking, the millions of words used in discussing, debating, demonstrating, arguing, made us yearn for a single expression of our complex educational philosophy. I struggled mightily to put it into words in all the inevitable speeches. But one night, after a speech at a parents meeting, I read a poem by Walt Whitman that must come as close as words can come, for parents and teachers have asked me to recite it again, year after year.

THERE WAS A CHILD WENT FORTH

There was a child went forth every day;
And the first object he look'd upon, that object he became;
And that object became part of him for the day, or a certain
    part of the day, or for many years, or stretching cycles
    of years.
The early lilacs became part of this child,
And grass, and white and red morning-glories, and white and
    red clover, and the song of the Phoebe-bird,
And the Third-month lambs, and the sow's pink-faint litter,
    and the mare's foal, and the cow's calf,
And the noisy brood of the barn-yard, or by the mire of the
    pond-side,
And the fish suspending themselves so curiously below there—
    and the beautiful curious liquid,
And the water-plants with their graceful flat heads—all
    became part of him.

134

The field-sprouts of April and May became part of him;
Winter-grain sprouts, and those of the light-yellow corn,
    and the esculent roots of the garden,
And the apple-trees cover'd with blossoms, and the fruit
    afterward, and wood-berries, and the commonest weeds
    by the road;
And the old drunkard staggering home from the out-house of
    the tavern, whence he had lately risen,
And the school-mistress that pass'd on her way to the school,
And the friendly boys that pass'd—and the quarrelsome boys,
And the tidy and fresh-cheek'd girls—and the barefoot negro
    boy and girl,
And all the changes of city and country, wherever he went.
His own parents,
He that had father'd him, and she that had conceiv'd him in
    her womb, and birth'd him,
They gave this child more of themselves than that;
They gave him afterward every day—they became part of him.
The mother at home, quietly placing the dishes on the supper-
    table;
The mother with mild words—clean her cap and gown, a wholesome
    odor falling off her person and clothes as she walks by;
The father, strong, self-sufficient, manly, mean, anger'd,
    unjust;
The blow, the quick loud word, the tight bargain, the crafty
    lure,
The family usages, the language, the company, the furniture—
    the yearning and swelling heart,
Affection that will not be gainsay'd—the sense of what is real—
    the thought, if, after all, it should prove unreal,
The doubts of day-time and the doubts of night-time—the
    curious whether and how,
Whether that which appears so is so, or is it all flashes
    and specks?
Men and women crowding fast in the streets—if they are not
    flashes and specks, what are they?
The streets themselves, and the façades of houses, and goods
    in the windows.
Vehicles, teams, the heavy-plank'd wharves—the huge crossing
    at the ferries,
The village on the highland, seen from afar at sunset—the
    river between,
Shadows, aureola and mist, the light falling on roofs and
    gables of white or brown, three miles off,
The schooner near by, sleepily dropping down the tide—the
    little boat slack-tow'd astern,
The hurrying tumbling waves, quick-broken crests, slapping,
The strata of color'd clouds, the long bar of maroon tint, away
    solitary by itself—the spread of purity it lies motionless in.
The horizon's edge, the flying sea-crow, the fragrance of
    salt marsh and shore mud;
These became part of that child who went forth every day,
    and who now goes, and will always go forth every day.

Walt Whitman *

* Leaves of Grass (David McKay, 1900).

17

A RECOLLECTION

Patrick Beatts*

We went to see the autogyro go up and come down again. An autogyro has a big, four-bladed propeller on the top so it can go up straighter than an airplane, and can come down in a smaller space.

It stayed down for a while and then went up again. It was in a big field on Baltimore Pike between Media and Swarthmore. It was Airmail Week and the autogyro was going to take some mail to Philly.

THE STORY ABOVE is a contribution to *Leaves* from two children in Eloise Holmes' group (eights and nines) circa 1942. It is almost a perfect example of good news-reporting, as you can see by eliminating sentence after sentence from the last one forward; you will find that you still have a complete piece of writing; second, it answers all six important questions—who, what, when, how and why; third, the children were writing simply, clearly, concisely. I have used this sample of writing for twelve years with groups of managers, engineers, and research people in a large corporation, as a part of courses on writing and communication. Usually, after some discussion, and generally with hesitancy, a few of the bolder ones ask if, "perhaps this was written by a child?"

So much for literacy at Rose Valley. Let us turn to art. Here I have long ago lost the original, carried for years in my wallet; but a verbal description may serve. One of my own group, the eleven- and twelve-year-olds, now a happily married Ph.D. with several children of her own, drew a cartoon for *Leaves*. The picture showed

* Pat Beatts was the teacher of the seventh and eighth grade group in the forties. He is now Education Research Administrator, Data Processing Division, IBM Corporation, Los Altos, California.

a residential street-corner with a large sign in the foreground reading, "DRIVE CAREFULLY, WE LOVE OUR CHILDREN." In the background was a window, shades drawn, and against them in silhouette, was a small child being thoroughly spanked by a parent.

Why is this worth mentioning? Because, knowing the artist, her parents, and the Rose Valley children, this was a sort of "in-house" joke over that "other world" that always exists in a real, or abstract, or general sense for people who have standards different from their times. The irony in the cartoon was light-hearted, lightly felt, and lightly expressed.

Art, almost by fiat, led us to music. The "oldest" group at Rose Valley, as they came to be called, knew "by heart" the words and music of some two hundred songs. They absorbed them rather than learned them. On a hiking trip to Cornwall Furnace, while they walked in heat and dust the eleven miles we had to walk because the bus had been cancelled on account of the war (World War II), they sang continuously for over an hour.

It was, however, not merely the Rose Valley atmosphere that produced this, but the tireless ebullience of our wonderful music teacher, Dorothy Hunt, who made music, all music, as natural a part of everyday life as eating or sleeping. We sang every day; and a large number of the group could and would play our piano!

Today the word is "relevance." How *relevant* was Rose Valley?

In history, one boy, a natural athlete but no scholar, became interested in the athletic and recreational contributions to life in the United States that various nations have contributed to America. He discovered, to his surprise and indignation, that no Negroes were then allowed in major league baseball. A year or so later he and another member of this group promoted and achieved the desegregation of both students and faculty at a prominent private boarding school. Here was activism before activism became as popular as it is today.

During three years, this group, beginning as ten-year-olds and ending as twelve-year-olds, planned and carried out an active athletic program of soccer, field-hockey, baseball, boxing, and an annual track and field day; they made cider; cleared an orchard to make an athletic field; helped build two new classrooms; went hiking and camping as far afield as Hershey, Pennsylvania; published a monthly magazine; visited all the Philadelphia museums, the Franklin Institute, and the children's concerts of the Philadelphia Orchestra; designed, arranged, and conducted our Friday evening "social affairs" at the school; acted as senior members on all the school's governing committees made up of two members of each class; supported a Spanish orphan; kept various pets ranging from hamsters to our goat called "Trinket"; performed the nativity play each Christmas in various versions; adapted or wrote one other play each year,

137

and performed the plays with scenery, costumes, props, lighting, and staging devised by themselves. All this in addition to "the regular curriculum." And all this without a single official homework assignment.

Sex has been a "problem" in American sixth to eighth grade levels for longer than one cares to remember. In my experience it was not a problem at Rose Valley. The interest or infatuation of girls and boys was taken for granted. The scene that comes back now was a class meeting, around 1943, when serious topics were in debate, and the boy who was chairman found attention wandering because one of the girls, had, as usual, taken the chair next to her current target, and was touching her knee to his. On appeal, which was the only legal means open to me to intervene, I said "————, stop flirting with ————!" The inevitable response was an indignant, "But I wasn't flirting!" at which the boy, her target, turned to her with a grin and said, "Well, what would you call it, then?" The meeting continued undisturbed when the laughter had subsided.

Incidentally, all the girls did shop-work, and all the boys took sewing and cooking; and the *Philadelphia Record* came out to photograph our mixed baseball (not softball) team.

A vital force at Rose Valley, "Mister," as everyone called Mr. Rawson, was in charge of shop work. At a long staff meeting during which I insisted that a soccer player in the second-oldest group be allowed to play against Penn Charter, contrary to our rules (those were the days of Gesell and age characteristics) my case was quietly won by Mister, who said, "You know, every time we make a rule we give up the chance of thinking."

Of course there were times when rules did have to be made and enforced. Occasionally it was the adults who forgot their place. One wet fall day a teacher was dashing from the main school to "the Chip." She was entering the end-door going directly into the nursery school, and was unaware that one of the boys in the oldest group was behind her, about to go around the long way in accordance with the rule that people must not go through the nursery school with dirty shoes, because the "littlest group" spend much of their time on the floor.

The boy told her she was breaking the rule, and, being late and frazzled, she replied that she was a teacher, to which the obvious answer came, "But your shoes are muddy just the same!" When she retorted and continued through the door, he followed. Of course, when she reported this insolence, the boy, and the rule, and the democratic process, and law and order were all upheld. There was no discrimination on account of age or sex at Rose Valley.

Perhaps the most fascinating, and certainly the most revealing, occurrence in my years at Rose Valley, from my viewpoint, was the

138

"authoritarian experiment." This occurred in the late fall of my first year at Rose Valley. Several of the group, then aged ten and eleven, had brothers or relatives who had gone on from Rose Valley to the local public schools. These older students would chide their younger brothers still at our school for not being up to snuff in vital matters like arithmetic. The question came up in our weekly class meeting; the consensus was that I did not control the classroom so that the pupils could do serious work. Against my vote, it was determined that I should control the class.

That weekend I arranged the chairs and tables in the classroom in neat mathematical rows and arranged the seating alphabetically. On Monday morning I made sure the doors were locked, and prepared myself for action. At Rose Valley, a locked classroom door was a monstrosity!

Amidst the puzzled, and somewhat irritated outcries of those locked out, I lined the whole crew up in the corridor and demanded silence. Then I ceremoniously unlocked the door, made them file in, and relished the dumbfounded silence when the geometric table arrangement hit them. Just in time, as they were about to pull open table drawers to identify their own tables, I began to tell them where to sit. Again came outraged cries. I persevered until all were seated.

Next, one of the girls opened her drawer and started taking out a book, paper and pencil. It was the edge of doom. I reprimanded her and, in response to her sincerely bewildered cry (it *would* have to be the most serious-minded one of all!), steeling myself, I declared that I would tell them when to open and what to take out of their drawers.

From then on we became a "disciplined group." I locked and unlocked doors, even at recess; posted an official list of the order in which they must get their lunch trays; and controlled the class, even to the extent of not allowing speech without a raised hand.

Our next crisis came on Thursday, sacrosanct as the day of class meeting. I could have guessed the agenda! However when two of the pupils started to move tables, preparatory to our setting our chairs in the magic circle, I told them to stop and announced that only I could call class meetings. As for this day, there would be no meeting.

I guess that was the trigger. The adult grapevine over that weekend told me of dire things in store, from sheer disgust to mutters of rebellion. Fortunately, I was saved from what today is called a "confrontation." It happened quite by accident, because of one boy's remarkable sense of justice, rational behavior, and tolerance. He had been home sick during the "week that was." When he returned, he at once became a focal center; he was the one person who could now be told (as news) all that had happened.

Soon he had a long conversation with me, at which he stated clearly (at age eleven) an unassailable position: a) He had been absent when the original decision had been made; b) it was therefore not binding on him; c) he had no intention of putting up with such foolishness; d) he had no use for the majority vote (he was a birthright Friend); e) he insisted on a class meeting for Thursday. With a show of reluctance that I did not really feel, I agreed. Inwardly I was delighted both at this heaven-sent means for me to save face and the beautifully individualistic and mature way he was behaving.

At that meeting, he ran the session. It opened with a sense of purpose and an air of tension that I have not frequently experienced. It lasted well over an hour, and almost everyone spoke up but me. The final motion was put by the chairman. It was reworded several times until all agreed; in essence it affirmed that the first thing we must learn, ahead of any subject, is self-control.

In the next two and one-half years the pupils proved they meant it; and they impressed it notably on new members who joined us later.

I cannot possibly estimate how valuable the lessons, experiences, and influences of those children and those three years at Rose Valley have been to me in my teaching.

140

18

FINANCIAL NOTES

Norman Brown*

IN THE FORTY YEARS of its existence, finances at The School in Rose Valley has evolved from the desperate problems of survival to the more pleasant ones of choice of policy. Perhaps this is not surprising, for evolution of the school's finances may have been somewhat parallel to the shift in economic position of the group of college faculty members, doctors, other professionals and members of the upper middle class from which its parent body is largely drawn.

During the years before World War II, will power and dedication to an educational ideal were the essential elements that closed the gap between what had to be done and the cash that could be found to do it. These elements are still essential. The school could not possibly survive in its present form without the voluntary labors of its parents and the dedication of its professional staff. But just as the modern counterpart of a college professor, who worried in 1948 about how to provide at all for his family, may now ponder the choice between a larger house or a vacation abroad, so the school can now assume its survival and is more free to make financial decisions on the basis of the kind of school it wishes to be.

This is not to say that the school has solved its financial problems. Far from it—they are the most inflexible and time-consuming matters that are discussed by the Board, a constant rein on the principal, and there is no foreseeable prospect of change. The question, however, is less likely to be *"can* we raise tuition"—for experi-

---

* Lawyer; graduate of The School in Rose Valley, treasurer of the school board from 1953–67, currently president of the Board; father of four children in the school, three having graduated.

ence has tended to show that we can—but *"should* we raise tuition."

For the last twenty years 63 percent to 89 percent of all the budgets have been devoted to teachers' salaries and the average has been close to 75 percent. During that period the greater part of the school's income was derived from tuition and other fees, with a small but significant difference being made up by benefits and contributions. In these years the school was occasionally able to realize a small surplus from operations and with about equal frequency was confronted with a deficit. The net result was to balance receipts and disbursements within a few hundred dollars.

It would be misleadingly simple to explain the school's finances merely in terms of a budget that devoted almost three-quarters of total outgo to teachers' salaries and depended upon tuition and other charges to parents for 80 to 85 percent of income. Behind these ultimate results lie a variety of considerations.

Compensation for the Staff

Teaching salaries in the Philadelphia area have tended to be higher in the public school systems than in the private schools and the Board of The School in Rose Valley has always been painfully conscious that salaries paid at the school were low, even by the standards of other private schools in the area. Consistent efforts to improve this situation over the years have increased salaries about three-fold since 1950, but there were similar increases elsewhere and the relative position of the school in this matter has probably not changed substantially. How then has the school been able to attract and hold a competent staff? Certainly the main reason has been the opportunity to participate in an educational environment that could be duplicated, if at all, in few other places. This has tended to result in a staff composed principally of women whose husbands provide the main source of family income, but it has been remarkable how many such qualified women have appeared and have been happy to accept positions at the school at $2,000 or $3,000 less than they might have earned elsewhere. *Public schools mainly*

Although individual salaries have been low, the over-all expenditure for teachers' salaries, expressed on a per-student basis, would probably compare favorably with other private schools and might even be large by public school standards. This reflects the fact that the school has tended to have a relatively high ratio of staff members to students and the extra freedom and the extra assistance that this produces has been one of the strong factors that have made the school attractive to prospective teachers. Indeed, there have been years in which the Board has been advised by staff members that they would prefer to have available funds used to provide extra assistants instead of being used to increase their own salaries.

142

Tuition

Tuition is the inevitable corollary to the question of teachers' salaries. Tuition at the school has increased steadily since World War II with substantial increases occurring every two or three years. In general the charges have been somewhat less than those at the conventional private schools to the west and northwest of the city and a few dollars more than those of the only other private school in the immediate vicinity. Experience has tended to show that tuition increases do not result in a significant drop in enrollment, but each increase has been accompanied by much concern about the effect on the parent body.

When tuition has been raised the school has usually made special scholarship allowances for any parents who might feel compelled to withdraw their child by reason of the increase, and as a result it is doubtful that a significant number of families already in the school has been driven away. The greater concern has been with the unknown number of prospects who may simply not return after visiting the school and finding out that the tuition is more than they can reasonably afford. To some extent this situation can be dealt with by a generous scholarship policy, but there will always be a number of people—who may in the long run be the most valuable members of a community, based on the concept of shared parental responsibility—who would not care to begin their association with the school by requesting special consideration. There is no real way of knowing how many such parents there have been, but it is comforting to observe that the parent body continues to be heavily weighted toward people with strong commitment to education and lively intellectual awareness in a variety of fields.

During most of the post-war period the school has consciously avoided setting tuition and other fees at a sufficiently high level to cover all regular operating costs. Inevitably, there are some parents who are in a position to do more than others, and by reason of their gifts or services the school has been able to rely upon a small but significant income from benefits and contributions to close the gap between tuition and operating expenses. This has made it possible to keep tuition at a minimum, without causing less affluent parents to feel that they must request special aid, and at the same time has provided a channel for those parents who have the resources or time to make an extra contribution to the school's finances.

Many schools have a tuition scale that increases as the children progress through higher grades. The school has not used such a scale for many years. In part this reflects a strong demand for pre-school services, that developed during the 1950's, which resulted in greater enrollment pressure in those levels than in the first to sixth grade levels. In addition, it reflects the fact that the cost of maintaining a child in the preschool is at least as great as the cost of maintaining him in the grade levels and there seems to be no logical basis for a lower tuition for the younger children. Similarly, the charge for half-day students in the preschool has been about three-quarters of the full-day charge. Acceptance of a half-day student pre-empts a place that could otherwise be made available to a full-day student and the saving in costs during the part of the day remaining after the child leaves is not substantial.

The question of tuition should not be left without a word about the possible dangers of charging *too little*. It seems to be generally agreed that consumers at all social and economic levels often measure the quality of an article by its price, and there is probably no reason to assume that this is markedly different in the field of education. Even a progressive school, seeking to appeal to intellectually oriented parents with a geniuine interest in education, must create confidence in its prospective clientele, and this confidence may not be promoted if the tuition is too far below what is known to be charged by other schools.

Transportation

Originally, the school drew upon a local clientele and the children could either walk or be brought with relatively little effort by their parents. This soon began to change and before the school was ten years old it was operating a station wagon to pick up students from more outlying regions. It now runs four buses which bring in perhaps one-third of the students, some from as far as twelve miles away; and the entire question of transportation is an excellent example of an area where financial and educational considerations are closely intertwined.

Typically, the problem may begin when it is thought that one of the groups would be a better educational unit if it had more children. There are no local children but a certain child would be enrolled if transportation could be provided. This is probably not feasible for a single child, but there may be a temptation to say that if this parent can recruit several other children in the same general region the school would establish a bus route to service them. This raises the financial question of whether such a route is profitable to the school and the educational question of whether the quality of the school experience is really valuable for children who must travel a great distance to attend and who will return to a home environment in which it will be difficult for them to associate with their schoolmates. The latter question is beyond the scope of this note, but it has often given much serious concern, and there have been those at the school who have wondered whether, if the school and home experience should ideally be unified as much as possible, too much attention was being concentrated on the educational experience during school hours to the exclusion of the effect of returning a child to a distant home after school is over.

On the financial side, it was the school's original experience that buses could not be made to be entirely self-sufficient. There have never been enough children on a route for the school to operate large, conventional school buses. Instead, we have used smaller vehicles of the suburban carry-all or Volkswagen microbus type that can take between ten and fourteen children. Even these have sometimes required children at the end of a route to travel for as much as an hour each way. These vehicles cost about $2,500 each and have tended to last from three to four years before the cost of repairs became prohibitive. For most of the post-war period the policy was to establish a varying transportation charge, based on distance, that was sufficient to cover drivers' salaries, insurance, and other costs of operation and about half the cost of replacement. The other half of the replacement cost was charged against the school's general operating budget, which meant that it was borne by the parent body as a whole, the philosophy being that there was some benefit to the entire school through having the larger student body produced by the buses.

Recently transportation charges have been increased and the school's latest budget shows the transportation fund as entirely self-sufficient.

Because of the school's location with respect to existing public school districts, it has not been possible to make any significant use of public school transportation which is available to students who can use existing public school bus routes. Other local private schools with a geographical situation that is better suited to this purpose have been able to make at least some use of this resource.

The general experience of Philadelphia schools appears to indicate that the provision of at least some transportation is a necessity for any suburban private school that does not have convenient mass transportation and an extremely heavy enrollment pressure. Provision of transportation is, however, a problem, not only from the viewpoint of cost, but because of the responsibility that must be assumed by the school for the safety of the students that it transports and the administrative burden placed upon the school's staff to arrange routes and schedules, engage reliable drivers, make sure all the children get on the bus in the afternoon, notify the driver of special arrangements when a child is not coming back, cope with winter storms, etc. The prospects of increasing enrollment and the flattering appeal of a parent who is enthusiastic but just can't get her child to school are blandishments that are hard to resist, but the school's experience suggests that this is an area which should be entered cautiously.

145

Other Expense

One of the reasons the school has been able to devote so large a percentage of its expenditures to salaries has been its success in using volunteer labor to build and maintain the physical plant. The land on which the school is situated was donated, and the vast majority of the buildings and other improvements have been built by the parents. The cost of the materials for these projects, and the cost of the buildings themselves in those cases where the work has been contracted, have generally been handled by special capital fund drives outside the school's regular budget. However, it would have been completely impossible to build even a small fraction of the school's physical plant if it were not for the donated labor of the parents.

Beyond the cost of construction, the annual cost of maintenance, which would normally be a charge against regular income from tuition, etc., has been kept at a minimum by "putter days" and other occasions on which parents have come out to handle much of the maintenance around the school. Anything lacking in their parents' abilities as carpenters has been more than compensated for by the quality of the accompanying discussions, and a prospective parent can readily see that whatever else his tuition may be spent on, it will not be wasted on an elaborate building program.

School Lunch Program

The School has always provided lunches for all students. Although there is a separate lunch charge, this is not optional and is as real an expense to parents as the tuition. A substantial aid in holding this cost to a minimum has been the National School Lunch Program administered by the Department of Agriculture. This program, which is intended to provide federal funds and some surplus food for hot, nourishing lunches for school children, is available to private and parochial as well as public schools. Participating institutions may not charge more than a certain amount (40¢ per lunch as of September 1969) and the program must not be run at a profit in the sense that it produces a surplus available to meet other phases of the school's operation. Obviously, these financial standards require certain internal accounting procedures that are not entirely susceptible to objective measurement. For example, what part of the cost of maintenance of the school's physical plant should be charged to lunch? If employees in the lunch program also perform other duties, what part of their compensation should be charged to which function? In general, however, the school has found the government's representatives to be quite reasonable in their understanding of our accounting problems and we have had no difficulty staying within the prescribed limits. In past years the program has produced a cash subsidy toward the cost of lunch which we are now (September 1970) told is to be discontinued. However, a more important element has been the surplus food provided free of cost. We have never entered the food supplied in kind on our books at a specific figure, but it is obvious that it has provided an important fraction of the over-all cost of meals for the students.